Differential Processing Trair
Acoustic Ta:

by Kerry Winget

Skills	Ages
■ auditory processing	■ 6 through 12
■ listening	**Grades**
	■ 1 through 7

Evidence-Based Practice

■ The ability to process sounds, to discriminate them accurately, and to interpret them correctly are critical skills for speech and language development (Taylor-Goh, 2005).

■ Intervention for auditory processing disorders using direct skills remediation and auditory training should incorporate a bottom-up (acoustic signal and auditory training) approach (ASHA, 2005; Chermak & Musiek, 2002).

■ Auditory training activities should include acoustically controlled tasks of sound intensity, frequency, and duration discrimination, as well as sound pattern recognition and sound localization (ASHA, 2005; Chermak & Musiek, 2002).

■ Recognition of auditory information in background noise simulates functional listening requirements in the classroom, community, and home environments (ASHA, 2005).

Differential Processing Training Program Acoustic Tasks incorporates these principles and is also based on expert professional practice.

References

American Speech-Language-Hearing Association (ASHA). (2005). *(Central) auditory processing disorders* [Technical Report]. Retrieved February 10, 2010, from www.asha.org/docs/pdf/TR2005-00043.pdf

Chermak, G.D., & Musiek, F.E. (2002). Auditory training: Principles and approaches for remediating and managing auditory processing disorders. *Seminars in Hearing, 23*, 297-308.

Taylor-Goh, S. (2005). *Royal college of speech & language therapists clinical guidelines.* United Kingdom: Speechmark.

LinguiSystems

LinguiSystems, Inc.
3100 4th Avenue
East Moline, IL 61244
800-776-4332

FAX: 800-577-4555
Email: service@linguisystems.com
Web: linguisystems.com

Copyright © 2007 LinguiSystems, Inc.

All of our products are copyrighted to protect the fine work of our authors. You may copy the task pages only as needed for your own use with clients. Any other reproduction or distribution of the pages in this book is prohibited, including copying the entire book to use as another primary source or "master" copy.

Printed in the U.S.A.
ISBN 978-0-7606-0722-0

About the Author

Kerry Winget, AuD, CCC-SLP/A, received her graduate training in speech-language pathology and audiology from Western Illinois University and her doctorate in audiology from the University of Florida. She has provided speech services in a variety of settings, including acute and rehabilitation hospitals, outpatient clinics, and public school systems, as well as audiological services in a private practice office and outpatient hospital clinic.

The Differential Processing Training Program is Kerry's first publication with LinguiSystems.

Dedication

To my parents and my husband for their love, patience, and support

Edited by Barb Truman
Page Layout by Jamie Bellagamba
Cover Design by Jeff Taylor

Table of Contents

Table of Contents, *continued*

Section Three: Auditory Discrimination

Unit One: Vowel Contrasts

Unit Two: Consonant Contrasts

Table of Contents, *continued*

Unit Three: Compound Word Contrasts

Unit Four: Auditory Vigilance

References

Introduction

Speech-language pathologists are seeing more and more students referred for suspected auditory processing difficulties. Referrals made by the classroom teacher may describe a student with difficulty following verbal instructions and sequential directions, distractibility, inconsistent academic performance, poor spelling and reading skills, and/or poor participation in group work. These types of behaviors, however, are common across a variety of diagnoses, including auditory processing, attention deficit, and specific language disorders. Effective screening and evaluation procedures help define the student's location of breakdown in auditory to linguistic processing ability, allowing more productive use of treatment time with focused treatment materials. Available instruments include *Differential Screening Test for Processing* (LinguiSystems, Inc.), *SCAN-C: Test for Auditory Processing Disorders in Children* (Harcourt Assessment, Inc.), and *Test of Auditory-Perceptual Skills-Revised (TAPS-R)* (Psychological and Educational Publications, Inc.).

There are three books in the *Differential Processing Training Program*:

- *Differential Processing Training Program: Acoustic Tasks*
- *Differential Processing Training Program: Acoustic-Linguistic Tasks*
- *Differential Processing Training Program: Linguistic Tasks*

These books contain sets of tasks developed to provide hierarchical practice across the continuum of auditory and linguistic processing. Used together, they provide material to strengthen the auditory foundations of basic sound difference awareness, manipulating those skills in sound and letter use, and finally mastering those skills in prosodic features and language efficiency. Each book may be used in isolation or in the continuum of related skills at that processing level.

Differential Processing Training Program: Acoustic Tasks is divided into three sections: Dichotic Listening, Temporal Patterning, and Auditory Discrimination. Each section provides tasks arranged in a hierarchy for effective auditory processing practice. Each task uses increasing auditory awareness and attention, helping to strengthen the child's overall active listening abilities.

There are a variety of treatment materials currently available that address various parts of the central auditory processing skills spectrum. The goal of the three books in the *Differential Processing Training Program* is to give the speech-language pathologist a range of related materials to use with all children with language processing difficulties, regardless of whether those difficulties begin with non-linguistic or linguistic language performance.

The *Differential Processing Training Program* was designed to help expand therapy resources for processing, from both the auditory and linguistic perspectives. I hope you find these exercises as exciting and effective as my clients have.

Kerry

Dichotic listening refers to the brain's ability to recognize different sounds from each ear even if they are heard at the exact same time. This means that the sounds in the right ear mean different things than the sounds in the left ear. The brain interprets each ear's message independently, instead of integrating the sounds into one meaning.

The majority of our everyday listening is binaural listening (both ears working together). By using both ears together, any sound information missed by one ear can be filled in by the other ear due to the redundancy of the auditory nervous system. We use these binaural skills to improve our hearing when there is more than one person talking or when we're listening in noisy places. The brain also uses binaural listening to help us locate where sounds are coming from, as the ear closest to the sound hears it fractions of a second before the other ear does.

Students with difficulties understanding auditory information when there is background noise or more than one person speaking at a time may benefit from specific training in dichotic and binaural listening skills. Dichotic tasks will help strengthen both auditory pathways individually. Binaural tasks will help strengthen auditory pathway integration.

The tasks in this section focus on training auditory listening skills for each ear separately, both ears together, and then both ears in opposition. Students use simple number repetition to learn the skill, and later expand on the skill using words and/or phrase repetition.

Presentation of Tasks

Students should initially learn auditory skills in a quiet setting, free from both auditory and visual distractions. Once proficiency is mastered, the students may practice in the presence of background noise, first in steady background noise and then in variable background noise. Steady background noise is often encountered in the classroom with ventilation units, fans, and electrical equipment hum. Variable background noise includes desk or paper shuffling, pencil-sharpening, group work activities, and any situation where more than one person is talking at a time. Both of these noise conditions increase the challenge of listening and may overwhelm a student who already struggles with hearing speech.

Unit One: Binaural Listening—The tasks in this section are designed with this quiet to noise hierarchy in mind. You can easily add steady background noise to any task by tuning a radio to static. Turn the noise to a level just softer than your voice. You can create variable background noise by tuning the radio to a station. As individual students differ in skills, try using a talk-radio station and then a music station. Again, turn the noise to a level just softer than your voice.

Unit Two: Monaural Listening and Unit Three: Monaural Alternating Listening—Due to the acoustic requirements of both monaural and monaural alternating listening, these tasks are recorded on the enclosed audio CD. To complete these tasks, you'll need a CD player with a headphone jack, two sets of stereo headphones, and a Y-cord adapter (available at local electronic stores). The instructions and the stimuli are on the CD and also printed in the manual. Both you and the student should wear stereo headphones connected with a Y-cord adapter.

Unit Four: Listening Localization—Provide the student with a blindfold, large hat, or blackened glasses so that he is unable to see you. For close distance tasks, stand within two to three steps of the student at the location indicated. For far distance tasks, stand within six to eight steps of the student. For all the tasks, as you change positions, be careful to move quietly so the student does not benefit from nonverbal auditory cues. For tasks with noise, position the noise any direction from the student and at the same distance from the student as you will be standing. If you wish, you can do a sound warm-up. Move the noise from position to position and have the student point to where he hears the noise. You can easily add steady background noise to any task by tuning a radio to static. Turn the noise to a level just softer than your voice. You can create variable background noise by tuning the radio to a station. As individual students differ in skills, try using a talk-radio station and then a music station. Again, turn the noise to a level just softer than your voice.

Unit Five: Dichotic Listening—Due to the acoustic requirements of dichotic listening, these tasks are recorded on the enclosed audio CD and must be conducted using stereo headphones. To complete these tasks, you'll need a CD player with a headphone jack, two sets of stereo headphones, and a Y-cord adapter (available at local electronic stores). The instructions and the stimuli are on the CD and also printed in the manual. Both you and the student should wear stereo headphones connected with a Y-cord adapter.

All Units—For all tasks, a specific goal is listed on each practice page. A performance grid is also provided on each page to track student performance. Mark a + for each correct answer and a – for each incorrect response. Monitor errors for any pattern and adjust material accordingly.

Section One: Dichotic Listening

Copyright © 2007 LinguiSystems, Inc.
Differential Processing Training Program: Acoustic Tasks

Task A: One- and Two-Digit Repetition

Goal: The student will repeat binaural numbers in quiet with 90% or greater accuracy.

You will hear a number. Say the number you hear.

	Dates				
1.	5				
2.	3				
3.	7				
4.	1				
5.	9				
6.	4				
7.	8				
8.	10				
9.	6				
10.	2				

Now listen for two numbers. Say the numbers in the order you hear them.

11.	1	5				
12.	8	3				
13.	6	8				
14.	9	2				
15.	7	1				
16.	10	4				
17.	3	9				
18.	5	6				
19.	4	7				
20.	2	10				
			20 %	20 %	20 %	20 %

Observations:

Task B: Three-Digit Repetition

Goal: The student will repeat binaural numbers in quiet with 90% or greater accuracy.

You will hear three numbers. Say the numbers in the order you hear them.

	Dates				
1.	5 2 9				
2.	6 9 3				
3.	8 4 6				
4.	3 5 8				
5.	10 3 5				
6.	7 8 3				
7.	2 1 4				
8.	9 6 10				
9.	1 9 7				
10.	4 7 2				
11.	6 10 1				
12.	4 3 9				
13.	2 8 10				
14.	3 7 4				
15.	8 1 5				
16.	10 2 8				
17.	5 6 2				
18.	1 4 7				
19.	9 10 6				
20.	7 5 1				
		20 %	20 %	20 %	20 %

Observations:

Task C: Four-Digit Repetition

Goal: The student will repeat binaural numbers in quiet with 90% or greater accuracy.

You will hear four numbers. Say the numbers in the order you hear them.

	Dates				
1.	9 5 3 2				
2.	8 4 10 5				
3.	3 8 9 6				
4.	6 2 1 10				
5.	1 7 6 9				
6.	10 3 5 3				
7.	2 6 7 1				
8.	4 1 2 7				
9.	5 10 4 8				
10.	7 9 8 4				
11.	10 6 4 3				
12.	9 5 1 6				
13.	4 9 10 7				
14.	7 3 2 1				
15.	2 8 7 10				
16.	1 4 6 4				
17.	3 7 8 2				
18.	6 1 5 9				
19.	8 10 9 5				
20.	5 2 3 9				
		20	20	20	20
		%	%	%	%

Observations:

Task D: One- and Two-Digit Repetition in Noise

Goal: The student will repeat binaural numbers in noise with 90% or greater accuracy.

You will hear a number and some noise. Say the number you hear.

Dates					
1.	9				
2.	3				
3.	6				
4.	1				
5.	5				
6.	4				
7.	8				
8.	10				
9.	7				
10.	2				

Now listen for two numbers. Say the numbers in the order you hear them.

11.	8	8				
12.	6	3				
13.	9	5				
14.	7	2				
15.	10	4				
16.	3	1				
17.	5	9				
18.	4	7				
19.	2	7				
20.	1	10				
			20	20	20	20
			%	%	%	%

Observations:

Dichotic Listening
Copyright © 2007 LinguiSystems, Inc.
Unit One: Binaural Listening
Differential Processing Training Program: Acoustic Tasks

Task E: Three-Digit Repetition in Noise

Goal: The student will repeat binaural numbers in noise with 90% or greater accuracy.

You will hear three numbers and some noise. Say the numbers in the order you hear them.

	Dates				
1.	9 5 2				
2.	6 8 4				
3.	8 3 5				
4.	5 10 3				
5.	3 7 8				
6.	4 2 1				
7.	10 9 6				
8.	7 1 9				
9.	2 4 7				
10.	1 6 10				
11.	9 4 3				
12.	10 2 8				
13.	4 3 7				
14.	5 8 1				
15.	8 10 2				
16.	2 5 6				
17.	7 1 4				
18.	6 9 10				
19.	1 7 5				
20.	3 6 9				
		20 %	20 %	20 %	20 %

Observations:

Task F: Four-Digit Repetition in Noise

Goal: The student will repeat binaural numbers in noise with 90% or greater accuracy.

You will hear four numbers and some noise. Say the numbers in the order you hear them.

	Dates				
1.	3 2 9 5				
2.	10 5 8 4				
3.	9 6 3 8				
4.	1 10 6 2				
5.	6 9 1 7				
6.	5 3 10 3				
7.	7 1 2 6				
8.	2 7 4 1				
9.	4 8 5 10				
10.	8 4 7 9				
11.	4 3 10 6				
12.	1 6 9 5				
13.	10 7 4 9				
14.	2 1 7 3				
15.	7 10 2 8				
16.	6 4 1 4				
17.	3 7 8 2				
18.	5 9 6 1				
19.	9 5 8 10				
20.	3 9 5 2				
		20 %	20 %	20 %	20 %

Observations:

Task A: One- to Four-Digit Repetition—Right Ear

Goal: The student will repeat monaural numbers in quiet with 90% or greater accuracy.

Instructions on CD (track 1): You will hear a number in your right ear. Point to your right ear. (Short pause) Say the number you hear.

	Dates				
1.	5				
2.	2				
3.	9				
4.	10				
5.	6				

Now listen for two numbers. Say the numbers in the order you hear them.

6.	1	5				
7.	9	3				
8.	4	8				
9.	6	2				
10.	7	10				

Now listen for three numbers. Say the numbers in the order you hear them.

11.	5	1	10				
12.	2	8	6				
13.	1	5	3				
14.	4	9	7				
15.	10	3	2				

Now listen for four numbers. Say the numbers in the order you hear them.

16.	1	4	5	7				
17.	9	2	7	6				
18.	3	8	2	10				
19.	4	9	6	3				
20.	5	10	8	1				
					20	20	20	20
					%	%	%	%

Task B: One- to Four-Digit Repetition—Left Ear

Goal: The student will repeat monaural numbers in quiet with 90% or greater accuracy.

Instructions on CD (track 2): You will hear a number in your left ear. Point to your left ear. (Short pause) Say the number you hear.

	Dates				
1.	3				
2.	8				
3.	7				
4.	5				
5.	1				

Now listen for two numbers. Say the numbers in the order you hear them.

6.	4	8				
7.	9	3				
8.	7	10				
9.	5	1				
10.	2	6				

Now listen for three numbers. Say the numbers in the order you hear them.

11.	3	1	9				
12.	6	4	10				
13.	2	7	5				
14.	1	8	3				
15.	9	2	4				

Now listen for four numbers. Say the numbers in the order you hear them.

16.	3	2	9	5				
17.	10	7	4	1				
18.	2	8	5	9				
19.	1	6	10	4				
20.	3	10	6	7				
					20	20	20	20
					%	%	%	%

Task C: One- to Four-Digit Repetition in Noise—Right Ear

Goal: The student will repeat monaural numbers in noise with 90% or greater accuracy.

Instructions on CD (track 3): You will hear a number and some noise in your right ear. Point to your right ear. (Short pause) Say the number you hear.

Dates				
1.	2			
2.	5			
3.	9			
4.	10			
5.	6			

Now listen for two numbers. Say the numbers in the order you hear them.

6.	10	5			
7.	4	3			
8.	9	8			
9.	6	2			
10.	7	1			

Now listen for three numbers. Say the numbers in the order you hear them.

11.	4	1	5		
12.	6	8	2		
13.	3	5	1		
14.	7	9	3		
15.	2	3	10		

Now listen for four numbers. Say the numbers in the order you hear them.

16.	5	7	1	4	
17.	8	6	9	2	
18.	2	10	3	8	
19.	6	9	4	7	
20.	3	1	5	10	

	/20	/20	/20	/20
	%	%	%	%

Task D: One- to Four-Digit Repetition in Noise—Left Ear

Goal: The student will repeat monaural numbers in noise with 90% or greater accuracy.

Instructions on CD (track 4): You will hear a number and some noise in your left ear. Point to your left ear. (Short pause) Say the number you hear.

Dates				
1. 3				
2. 8				
3. 7				
4. 5				
5. 1				

Now listen for two numbers. Say the numbers in the order you hear them.

6. 4 8				
7. 1 9				
8. 7 10				
9. 5 3				
10. 2 6				

Now listen for three numbers. Say the numbers in the order you hear them.

11. 7 4 10				
12. 3 1 9				
13. 2 7 5				
14. 9 2 4				
15. 1 8 3				

Now listen for four numbers. Say the numbers in the order you hear them.

16. 9 7 4 1				
17. 5 10 3 2				
18. 3 8 6 7				
19. 4 6 5 9				
20. 1 2 10 4				
	20	20	20	20
	%	%	%	%

Task A: Two- to Four-Digit Repetition

Goal: The student will repeat monaural alternated numbers in quiet with 90% or greater accuracy.

Instructions on CD (track 5): You will hear a number in your right ear and another number in your left ear. Say the numbers in the order you hear them.

			Dates				
	Right	*Left*					
1.	2	4					
2.	3	9					
3.	10	6					

Now listen for three numbers. Say the numbers in the order you hear them.

	Right	*Left*	*Right*				
4.	3	5	7				
5.	9	3	10				
6.	2	4	8				

Now listen for four numbers. Say the numbers in the order you hear them.

	Right	*Left*	*Right*	*Left*			
7.	5	1	8	7			
8.	7	6	10	5			
9.	3	9	1	4			
10.	2	8	4	6			

(continued on next page)

Observations:

Task A: Two- to Four-Digit Repetition, *continued*

Now you will hear a number in your left ear and another number in your right ear. Say the numbers in the order you hear them.

	Left	Right				
11.	3	9				
12.	5	7				
13.	6	1				

Now listen for three numbers. Say the numbers in the order you hear them.

	Left	Right	Left				
14.	6	5	7				
15.	3	1	8				
16.	2	9	6				

Now listen for four numbers. Say the numbers in the order you hear them.

	Left	Right	Left	Right				
17.	4	3	2	9				
18.	10	5	8	3				
19.	1	4	7	5				
20.	2	8	10	6				
					20	20	20	20
					%	%	%	%

Observations:

Task B: Two- to Four-Digit Repetition in Noise

Goal: The student will repeat monaural alternated numbers in noise with 90% or greater accuracy.

Instructions on CD (track 6): You will hear a number in your right ear and another number in your left ear. You will also hear some noise. Say the numbers in the order you hear them.

	Dates					
	Right	Left				
1.	10	6				
2.	3	5				
3.	2	9				

Now listen for three numbers. Say the numbers in the order you hear them.

	Right	Left	Right				
4.	2	4	6				
5.	3	5	10				
6.	7	8	1				

Now listen for four numbers. Say the numbers in the order you hear them.

	Right	Left	Right	Left			
7.	8	2	10	3			
8.	2	7	6	4			
9.	5	1	7	8			
10.	6	9	5	10			

(continued on next page)

Observations:

Task B: Two- to Four-Digit Repetition in Noise, *continued*

Now you will hear a number in your left ear and another number in your right ear. You will also hear some noise. Say the numbers in the order you hear them.

	Left	Right				
11.	6	1				
12.	3	7				
13.	5	9				

Now listen for three numbers. Say the numbers in the order you hear them.

	Left	Right	Left				
14.	4	7	3				
15.	5	2	6				
16.	1	9	8				

Now listen for four numbers. Say the numbers in the order you hear them.

	Left	Right	Left	Right				
17.	1	5	3	7				
18.	3	4	2	9				
19.	8	2	10	6				
20.	5	10	8	1				
					20	20	20	20
					%	%	%	%

Observations:

Dichotic Listening
Copyright © 2007 LinguiSystems, Inc.

Unit Three: Monaural Alternating Listening
Differential Processing Training Program: Acoustic Tasks

Task C: Sentence Repetition

Goal: The student will repeat monaural alternated words in quiet with 90% or greater accuracy.

Instructions on CD (track 7): You will hear words in your right ear and words in your left ear. Say the sentence you hear.

	Right	Left	Right	Left	Dates			
1.	The	coat	was	blue.				
2.	Her	hat	was	lost.				
3.	Many	kids	like	tennis.				
4.	Apples	make	good	pies.				
5.	Rake	the	fall	leaves.				
6.	Dogs	chased	the	cat.				
7.	The	red	flowers	grew.				
8.	Most	pencils	have	erasers.				
9.	The	horn	was	loud.				
10.	His	coat	was	green.				

	Right	Left	Right	Left	Right	Left			
11.	We	have	art	and	gym	today.			
12.	They	ate	salad	with	ranch	dressing.			
13.	The	bags	were	heavy	with	candy.			
14.	Rain	fell	on	the	red	car.			
15.	His	feet	left	big	wet	footprints.			
16.	She	saw	bees	and	bugs	today.			
17.	Fires	make	lots	of	thick	smoke.			
18.	Boats	sailed	on	the	blue	water.			
19.	He	fell	and	broke	his	glasses.			
20.	She	took	the	cake	to	school.			
							20	20	20	20
							%	%	%	%

Observations:

Task D: Sentence Repetition in Noise

Goal: The student will repeat monaural alternated words in noise with 90% or greater accuracy.

Instructions on CD (track 8): You will hear words in your right ear and words in your left ear. You will also hear some noise. Say the sentence you hear.

	Right	Left	Right	Left	Dates			
1.	Her	hat	fell	off.				
2.	Cats	chased	the	bird.				
3.	The	baby	wore	pants.				
4.	Nuts	are	good	snacks.				
5.	Build	a	new	house.				
6.	The	dog	had	fleas.				
7.	The	TV	was	downstairs.				
8.	Don't	wake	the	baby.				
9.	Go	out	and	play.				
10.	The	pen	leaked	everywhere.				

	Right	Left	Right	Left	Right	Left				
11.	The	mouse	went	inside	the	house.				
12.	Feel	the	big	soft	fur	blanket.				
13.	She	read	the	new	library	book.				
14.	He	drove	the	car	on	vacation.				
15.	The	light	bulb	was	burned	out.				
16.	The	berry	did	not	taste	good.				
17.	It's	too	heavy	to	lift	up.				
18.	The	gift	was	on	the	porch.				
19.	Chalk	can	leave	white	dust	everywhere.				
20.	Socks	keep	your	feet	toasty	warm.				
							/20 %	/20 %	/20 %	/20 %

Observations:

Task A: Word Localization at a Close Distance

Goal: The student will indicate where he hears target words in quiet with 90% or greater accuracy.

You will hear words coming from different places. Point to where you hear each word.

	Dates				
1.	(in front) scarecrow				
2.	(behind) cake pan				
3.	(to the left) acorn				
4.	(in front) sunset				
5.	(to the right) popcorn				
6.	(to the left) rainbow				
7.	(behind) snowman				
8.	(to the right) armchair				
9.	(behind) sidewalk				
10.	(in front) hot dog				
11.	(in front) grapevine				
12.	(to the left) heat wave				
13.	(to the right) baseball				
14.	(to the left) duck pond				
15.	(behind) drawbridge				
16.	(to the left) playground				
17.	(behind) toothbrush				
18.	(in front) cookbook				
19.	(to the left) lifeboat				
20.	(in front) mushroom				
		20	20	20	20
		%	%	%	%

Observations:

Task B: Word Localization at a Far Distance

Goal: The student will indicate where he hears target words in quiet with 90% or greater accuracy.

You will hear words coming from different places. Point to where you hear each word.

	Dates				
1.	(behind)	shipwreck			
2.	(in front)	inkwell			
3.	(to the right)	starlight			
4.	(in front)	platform			
5.	(to the left)	birthday			
6.	(to the right)	ice cream			
7.	(in front)	mushroom			
8.	(to the right)	northwest			
9.	(behind)	buckwheat			
10.	(in front)	cookbook			
11.	(in front)	washboard			
12.	(to the left)	heat wave			
13.	(to the right)	baseball			
14.	(to the left)	duck pond			
15.	(behind)	drawbridge			
16.	(to the left)	playground			
17.	(behind)	toothbrush			
18.	(in front)	bird's nest			
19.	(to the left)	lifeboat			
20.	(behind)	eggplant			
			20	20	20	20
			%	%	%	%

Observations:

Task C: Word Localization at a Close Distance in Steady Noise

Goal: The student will indicate where he hears target words in steady noise with 90% or greater accuracy.

You will hear words coming from different places. You will also hear some noise. Point to where you hear each word.

	Dates				
1.	(behind)	shipwreck				
2.	(to the right)	northwest				
3.	(in front)	inkwell				
4.	(to the left)	birthday				
5.	(to the right)	ice cream				
6.	(in front)	platform				
7.	(in front)	mushroom				
8.	(to the right)	starlight				
9.	(in front)	cookbook				
10.	(behind)	buckwheat				
11.	(in front)	washboard				
12.	(to the left)	heat wave				
13.	(to the right)	baseball				
14.	(behind)	drawbridge				
15.	(to the left)	duck pond				
16.	(to the left)	playground				
17.	(behind)	toothbrush				
18.	(behind)	eggplant				
19.	(to the left)	lifeboat				
20.	(in front)	bird's nest				
			20	20	20	20
			%	%	%	%

Observations:

Task D: Word Localization at a Far Distance in Steady Noise

Goal: The student will indicate where he hears target words in steady noise with 90% or greater accuracy.

You will hear words coming from different places. You will also hear some noise. Point to where you hear each word.

	Dates				
1.	(behind) wheelchair				
2.	(to the right) sidewalk				
3.	(in front) inkwell				
4.	(to the left) heat wave				
5.	(in front) cookbook				
6.	(in front) popcorn				
7.	(in front) mushroom				
8.	(to the right) starlight				
9.	(to the right) ice cream				
10.	(behind) buckwheat				
11.	(in front) washboard				
12.	(to the left) cake pan				
13.	(to the right) baseball				
14.	(behind) drawbridge				
15.	(to the left) duck pond				
16.	(behind) eggplant				
17.	(behind) toothbrush				
18.	(to the left) lifeboat				
19.	(to the left) playground				
20.	(in front) bird's nest				
		20	20	20	20
		%	%	%	%

Observations:

Task E: Word Repetition at a Close Distance

Goal: The student will repeat target words in quiet with 90% or greater accuracy.

You will hear words coming from different places. Say each word you hear.

	Dates				
1.	(behind)	snowman			
2.	(behind)	cake pan			
3.	(to the right)	acorn			
4.	(in front)	sunset			
5.	(to the left)	rainbow			
6.	(to the right)	popcorn			
7.	(in front)	scarecrow			
8.	(to the right)	armchair			
9.	(in front)	grapevine			
10.	(in front)	hot dog			
11.	(behind)	sidewalk			
12.	(to the left)	heat wave			
13.	(to the left)	duck pond			
14.	(to the right)	baseball			
15.	(behind)	drawbridge			
16.	(to the left)	playground			
17.	(behind)	toothbrush			
18.	(in front)	mushroom			
19.	(to the left)	lifeboat			
20.	(behind)	toothbrush			
			20	20	20	20
			%	%	%	%

Observations:

Task F: Word Repetition at a Far Distance

Goal: The student will repeat target words in quiet with 90% or greater accuracy.

You will hear words coming from different places. Say each word you hear.

		Dates				
1.	(to the right)	fire truck				
2.	(in front)	grapevine				
3.	(to the right)	acorn				
4.	(in front)	sunset				
5.	(to the left)	rainbow				
6.	(behind)	snowman				
7.	(in front)	scarecrow				
8.	(to the right)	armchair				
9.	(behind)	cake pan				
10.	(in front)	hot dog				
11.	(to the left)	duck pond				
12.	(to the right)	baseball				
13.	(to the left)	airplane				
14.	(behind)	sidewalk				
15.	(behind)	drawbridge				
16.	(to the left)	playground				
17.	(to the left)	lifeboat				
18.	(in front)	mushroom				
19.	(in front)	cookbook				
20.	(behind)	sailboat				
			20	20	20	20
			%	%	%	%

Observations:

Task G: Word Repetition at a Close Distance in Steady Noise

Goal: The student will repeat target words in steady noise with 90% or greater accuracy.

You will hear words coming from different places. You will also hear some noise. Say each word you hear.

	Dates				
1.	(behind) inkwell				
2.	(to the right) wristwatch				
3.	(in front) light bulb				
4.	(in front) cookbook				
5.	(to the right) ice cream				
6.	(in front) popcorn				
7.	(to the left) heat wave				
8.	(to the right) starlight				
9.	(in front) mushroom				
10.	(behind) hot wheels				
11.	(in front) washboard				
12.	(to the left) cake pan				
13.	(to the left) duck pond				
14.	(behind) drawbridge				
15.	(behind) earthworm				
16.	(to the right) baseball				
17.	(to the left) playground				
18.	(to the left) lifeboat				
19.	(behind) toothbrush				
20.	(in front) acorn				
		20	20	20	20
		%	%	%	%

Observations:

Task H: Word Repetition at a Far Distance in Steady Noise

Goal: The student will repeat target words in steady noise with 90% or greater accuracy.

You will hear words coming from different places. You will also hear some noise. Say each word you hear.

		Dates				
1.	(to the right)	notepad				
2.	(behind)	armchair				
3.	(in front)	light bulb				
4.	(to the left)	snowman				
5.	(in front)	popcorn				
6.	(to the right)	ice cream				
7.	(to the left)	heat wave				
8.	(to the right)	bathtub				
9.	(in front)	mushroom				
10.	(behind)	hot wheels				
11.	(in front)	washboard				
12.	(behind)	earthworm				
13.	(to the left)	duck pond				
14.	(behind)	drawbridge				
15.	(to the left)	wristwatch				
16.	(to the right)	baseball				
17.	(to the left)	playground				
18.	(to the left)	football				
19.	(behind)	toothbrush				
20.	(in front)	sailboat				
			20	20	20	20
			%	%	%	%

Observations:

Task I: Word Repetition at a Close Distance in Variable Noise

Goal: The student will repeat target words in noise with 90% or greater accuracy.

You will hear words coming from different places. You will also hear some noise. Say each word you hear.

		Dates				
1.	(to the right)	doorknob				
2.	(behind)	earthworm				
3.	(in front)	light bulb				
4.	(to the left)	snowman				
5.	(in front)	popcorn				
6.	(to the right)	ice cream				
7.	(to the left)	heat wave				
8.	(to the right)	bathtub				
9.	(in front)	mushroom				
10.	(behind)	farewell				
11.	(in front)	washboard				
12.	(behind)	scarecrow				
13.	(to the left)	duck pond				
14.	(behind)	drawbridge				
15.	(to the right)	wristwatch				
16.	(to the left)	football				
17.	(to the left)	playground				
18.	(to the right)	fireplace				
19.	(behind)	toothbrush				
20.	(in front)	sailboat				
			20	20	20	20
			%	%	%	%

Observations:

Task J: Word Repetition at a Far Distance in Variable Noise

Goal: The student will repeat target words in noise with 90% or greater accuracy.

You will hear words coming from different places. You will also hear some noise. Say each word you hear.

		Dates				
1.	(to the right)	shipwreck				
2.	(behind)	daybreak				
3.	(in front)	light bulb				
4.	(to the left)	snowman				
5.	(in front)	popcorn				
6.	(to the right)	ice cream				
7.	(to the left)	heat wave				
8.	(to the right)	bathtub				
9.	(in front)	fire truck				
10.	(behind)	fish tank				
11.	(in front)	washboard				
12.	(behind)	scarecrow				
13.	(to the left)	duck pond				
14.	(behind)	drawbridge				
15.	(to the right)	wristwatch				
16.	(to the left)	football				
17.	(to the left)	playground				
18.	(to the right)	fireplace				
19.	(behind)	toothbrush				
20.	(in front)	sailboat				
			20	20	20	20
			%	%	%	%

Observations:

Task A: One-Digit Repetition—Ear Selectivity

Goal: The student will repeat target numbers in quiet with 90% or greater accuracy.

Instructions on CD (track 9): You will hear a different number in each ear at the same time. Point to your right ear. (Short pause) Say the number you hear in your right ear only.

Dates						
	Left	*Right*				
1.	4	6				
2.	2	8				
3.	6	5				
4.	7	2				
5.	6	1				
6.	8	4				
7.	3	9				
8.	2	10				
9.	5	7				
10.	9	4				

Now point to your left ear. (Short pause) Say the number you hear in your left ear only.

	Left	*Right*				
11.	5	1				
12.	3	7				
13.	2	10				
14.	8	4				
15.	10	6				
16.	4	9				
17.	1	8				
18.	3	5				
19.	7	2				
20.	6	9				
			20	20	20	20
			%	%	%	%

Observations:

Task B: One-Digit Repetition in Noise—Ear Selectivity

Goal: The student will repeat target numbers in noise with 90% or greater accuracy.

Instructions on CD (track 10): You will hear a different number in each ear at the same time. You will also hear some noise. Point to your right ear. (Short pause) Say the number you hear in your right ear only.

	Dates					
	Left	*Right*				
1.	6	5				
2.	9	3				
3.	8	2				
4.	7	10				
5.	8	7				
6.	1	4				
7.	3	9				
8.	4	10				
9.	8	1				
10.	6	3				

Now point to your left ear. (Short pause) Say the number you hear in your left ear only.

	Left	*Right*				
11.	4	2				
12.	7	8				
13.	5	6				
14.	10	8				
15.	9	3				
16.	4	2				
17.	1	9				
18.	10	3				
19.	5	6				
20.	1	7				
			20	20	20	20
			%	%	%	%

Observations:

Task C: Two- and Four-Digit Repetition

Goal: The student will repeat dichotic numbers in quiet with 90% or greater accuracy.

Instructions on CD (track 11): You will hear a different number in each ear at the same time. Say the numbers you hear.

	Left	Right	Dates			
1.	1	5				
2.	9	2				
3.	8	4				
4.	7	6				
5.	5	1				
6.	3	10				
7.	4	7				
8.	2	9				
9.	10	8				
10.	6	3				

Now you will hear two numbers in each ear at the same time. Say the numbers you hear.

	Left	Right	Left	Right			
11.	3	5	9	8			
12.	5	3	4	10			
13.	8	1	2	6			
14.	4	9	1	3			
15.	10	2	3	5			
16.	2	8	6	7			
17.	9	4	8	2			
18.	7	6	10	1			
19.	1	7	5	4			
20.	6	10	7	9			
					20 / %	20 / %	20 / %

Observations:

Task D: Two- and Four-Digit Repetition in Noise

Goal: The student will repeat dichotic numbers in noise with 90% or greater accuracy.

Instructions on CD (track 12): You will hear a different number in each ear at the same time. You will also hear some noise. Say the numbers you hear.

	Left	Right	Dates			
1.	7	6				
2.	4	9				
3.	1	2				
4.	9	5				
5.	8	4				
6.	5	1				
7.	3	10				
8.	2	7				
9.	10	8				
10.	6	3				

Now you will hear two numbers in each ear at the same time. Say the numbers you hear.

	Left	Right	Left	Right			
11.	3	5	9	8			
12.	5	3	4	10			
13.	6	10	7	9			
14.	4	9	1	3			
15.	10	2	8	5			
16.	9	4	6	2			
17.	2	8	3	7			
18.	7	6	10	1			
19.	1	7	5	4			
20.	8	1	2	6			
					20	20	20	20
					%	%	%	%

Observations:

Task E: Two- and Four-Word Repetition

Goal: The student will repeat dichotic words in quiet with 90% or greater accuracy.

Instructions on CD (track 13): You will hear a different word in each ear at the same time. Say the words you hear.

	Left	Right	Dates			
1.	kiss	soap				
2.	face	boot				
3.	map	two				
4.	key	star				
5.	duck	lip				
6.	rope	game				
7.	fire	beep				
8.	goat	sail				
9.	feet	dip				
10.	book	white				

Now you will hear two words in each ear at the same time. Say the words you hear.

	Left	Right	Left	Right				
11.	like	toe	feet	duck				
12.	tank	corn	eye	rag				
13.	leaf	doll	bike	face				
14.	geese	up	loose	sack				
15.	vase	night	rope	cook				
16.	mad	day	desk	back				
17.	fish	coat	peach	knot				
18.	pit	hand	half	goat				
19.	pay	sheet	cat	tight				
20.	dog	air	red	big				
					20	20	20	20
					%	%	%	%

Observations:

Task F: Two- and Four-Word Repetition in Noise

Goal: The student will repeat dichotic words in noise with 90% or greater accuracy.

Instructions on CD (track 14): You will hear a different word in each ear at the same time. You will also hear some noise. Say the words you hear.

		Dates				
	Left	Right				
1.	hat	tan				
2.	laugh	book				
3.	key	ship				
4.	ball	feet				
5.	box	pail				
6.	rock	chalk				
7.	page	hit				
8.	pen	ear				
9.	camp	base				
10.	tent	coat				

Now you will hear two words in each ear at the same time. Say the words you hear.

	Left	Right	Left	Right				
11.	rush	loaf	tube	bath				
12.	four	tan	team	bite				
13.	red	leaf	find	rich				
14.	ham	root	tail	mash				
15.	rose	hat	blue	moth				
16.	lick	rope	top	wash				
17.	pink	off	half	comb				
18.	cuff	right	sock	leap				
19.	hook	fin	light	grass				
20.	read	pole	black	chew				
					20	20	20	20
					%	%	%	%

Observations:

Task G: Phrase and Sentence Repetition

Goal: The student will repeat dichotic phrases and sentences in quiet with 90% or greater accuracy.

Instructions on CD (track 15): You will hear a different phrase or sentence in each ear at the same time. Say the phrases and sentences you hear.

	Left	Right	Dates			
1.	Cold and wet	She ate cheese.				
2.	He went fishing.	A baseball game				
3.	The dog barked.	Tie the rope.				
4.	Cat and mouse	The balloon broke.				
5.	Three o'clock	Salt and pepper				
6.	Time to eat.	Ice-cream sundae				
7.	Pencil and paper	A spelling test				
8.	Meet after school.	Bees and honey				
9.	Hit the baseball.	Open the window.				
10.	Write the letter.	Eat the sandwich.				
11.	Hot and cold	Pack your bag.				
12.	Fold the paper.	Watch television.				
13.	The birds fly.	Clean your room.				
14.	Sun and moon	Loud and clear				
15.	Go to sleep.	Hold the phone.				
16.	Chew the gum.	Raise your hand.				
17.	Eggs and bacon	Close the door.				
18.	Meat and potatoes	The planet Earth				
19.	Throw the ball.	Up the stairs				
20.	Smell the flower.	Peel the sticker.				
			20	20	20	20
			%	%	%	%

Observations:

Task H: Phrase and Sentence Repetition in Noise

Goal: The student will repeat dichotic phrases and sentences in noise with 90% or greater accuracy.

Instructions on CD (track 16): You will hear a different phrase or sentence in each ear at the same time. You will also hear some noise. Say the phrases and sentences you hear.

	Left	Right	Dates			
1.	Eat the pie.	Pick the flower.				
2.	Say the number.	Write the letter.				
3.	Buy the shirt.	Red and white				
4.	Make the bed.	Hop and jump.				
5.	Spin the wheel.	Wash the dish.				
6.	Mow the grass.	Make popcorn.				
7.	Look and listen.	Paint two pictures.				
8.	Turn it over.	Play the piano.				
9.	A spelling bee	Laugh and smile.				
10.	Stub your toe.	Fly the kite.				
11.	Comb your hair.	Dogs and cats				
12.	He eats pudding.	Light the candle.				
13.	She drives cars.	Popcorn and peanuts				
14.	Make the dinner.	Cook and clean.				
15.	You know that.	Hat and coat				
16.	Shoes and socks	Wipe your hands.				
17.	Good and bad	Help me please.				
18.	Pet the dog.	Slam the door.				
19.	Turn it off.	Pots and pans				
20.	Ten blue pens	Clean your glasses.				
			20	20	20	20
			%	%	%	%

Observations:

Dichotic Listening
Copyright © 2007 LinguiSystems, Inc.
Unit Five: Dichotic Listening
Differential Processing Training Program: Acoustic Tasks

Temporal patterning refers to the awareness of acoustic patterns within sounds. Our ears use many features to differentiate sounds. Some sounds are low and booming, like a clap of thunder, and others are soft and rhythmic, like a ticking clock. Sounds may vary in their pitch or tone, loudness, and length. It is the combinations of these characteristics that make sounds unique and allow us to attach meaning to different sounds. Just as we learn that a telephone's dial tone is different from the busy signal, we use these same acoustic patterns to differentiate between the sounds of our language. A student who has difficulty identifying basic changes in sounds will have difficulty hearing the subtle acoustic changes of speech.

The sets of tasks in this section focus on temporal patterning for pitch, loudness, and duration variations. Each unit begins with tasks in discrimination, requiring the student to listen and decide if the sound patterns are the same or different. Later the student listens and then demonstrates the patterns independently.

Presentation of Tasks

Unit One: Pitch Variation—Use your voice or two noisemakers to make low and high pitches. Establish one pitch for the high sounds and another pitch for the low sounds. Make the sounds at a comfortable loudness level and hold the sounds for a consistent duration. If you use your voice, produce a neutral sound such as "ahhh." Effective noisemakers include bells, drums, or a keyboard. Use a consistent pace throughout the tasks, pausing briefly between presentations.

Unit Two: Loudness Variation—Use your voice or a noisemaker to make soft and loud sounds. Establish one level for the soft sounds and another level for the loud sounds. Hold the sounds for a consistent duration. Use a consistent pace throughout the tasks, pausing briefly between presentations.

Unit Three: Duration Variation—Use your voice or a noisemaker to make short and long sounds. Establish one length for short sounds and another length for long sounds. If you use your voice, a sibilant sound such as "sss" works well. Use a consistent pace throughout the tasks, pausing briefly between each sound.

All Units—Pause long enough (i.e., 2-4 seconds) between the first and second patterns so the student hears them as two units. A shorter pause will better reflect auditory discrimination; a longer pause will also task auditory memory skills.

Students should initially learn auditory skills in a quiet setting, free from both auditory and visual distractions. Once proficiency is mastered, the students may practice in the presence of background noise, first in steady background noise and then in variable background noise. Steady background noise is often encountered in the classroom with ventilation units, fans, and electrical equipment hum. Variable background noise includes desk or paper shuffling, pencil-sharpening, group work activities, and any situation where more than one person is talking at a time. Both of these noise conditions increase the challenge of listening and may overwhelm a student who already struggles with hearing speech.

The tasks in this section are designed with this quiet to noise hierarchy in mind. You can easily add steady background noise to the task by tuning a radio to static. Turn the noise to a level just softer than your voice/sounds. You can create variable background noise by tuning the radio to a station. As individual students differ in skills, try using a talk-radio station and then a music station. Again, turn the noise to a level just softer than your voice/ sounds.

A specific goal is listed on each practice page. A performance grid is also provided on each page to track student performance. Mark a + for each correct answer and a – for each incorrect response. Monitor errors for any pattern and adjust material accordingly.

Section Two: Temporal Patterning

Unit One: Pitch Variation

Unit Two: Loudness Variation

Copyright © 2007 LinguiSystems, Inc.
Differential Processing Training Program: Acoustic Tasks

Section Two: Temporal Patterning

Unit Three: Duration Variation

Task A: 1:1 Discrimination

Goal: The student will discriminate pitch matches in quiet with 90% or greater accuracy.

You will hear two sounds. Tell me if the sounds are the same (S) or different (D).

		Dates				
1.	High – High	(S)				
2.	Low – Low	(S)				
3.	Low – High	(D)				
4.	High – High	(S)				
5.	Low – Low	(S)				
6.	High – Low	(D)				
7.	Low – High	(D)				
8.	Low – Low	(S)				
9.	High – Low	(D)				
10.	Low – High	(D)				
11.	Low –Low	(S)				
12.	High – Low	(D)				
13.	Low – High	(D)				
14.	High – High	(S)				
15.	Low – High	(D)				
16.	High – High	(S)				
17.	High – Low	(D)				
18.	Low – Low	(S)				
19.	Low – High	(D)				
20.	High – High	(S)				
			20	20	20	20
			%	%	%	%

Observations:

Task B: 2:2 Discrimination

Goal: The student will discriminate pitch patterns in quiet with 90% or greater accuracy.

You will hear two sound patterns. Tell me if the patterns are the same (S) or different (D).

	Dates				
1.	High High – High High	(S)			
2.	Low High – High High	(D)			
3.	High Low – High Low	(S)			
4.	Low Low – Low Low	(S)			
5.	High Low – Low High	(D)			
6.	Low Low – High High	(D)			
7.	High High – Low High	(D)			
8.	Low Low – Low Low	(S)			
9.	High Low – High Low	(S)			
10.	High High – Low Low	(D)			
11.	Low High – Low Low	(D)			
12.	High High – High High	(S)			
13.	Low High – High High	(D)			
14.	High Low – High Low	(S)			
15.	Low Low – Low High	(D)			
16.	High High – High High	(S)			
17.	Low High – Low Low	(D)			
18.	High Low – Low Low	(D)			
19.	Low Low – Low Low	(S)			
20.	Low High – Low High	(S)			
			20	20	20	20
			%	%	%	%

Observations:

Task C: 3:3 Discrimination

Goal: The student will discriminate pitch patterns in quiet with 90% or greater accuracy.

You will hear two sound patterns. Tell me if the patterns are the same (S) or different (D).

	Dates				
1.	Low High Low – Low High Low	(S)			
2.	Low Low High – Low Low High	(S)			
3.	High High High – High Low Low	(D)			
4.	Low High High – Low High Low	(D)			
5.	High Low Low – High High Low	(D)			
6.	Low High High – Low High High	(S)			
7.	High Low Low – High Low High	(D)			
8.	Low Low Low – Low Low Low	(S)			
9.	High Low High – High Low Low	(D)			
10.	Low Low High – Low High High	(D)			
11.	High Low Low – High Low High	(D)			
12.	Low High High – Low High High	(S)			
13.	High High Low – High High Low	(S)			
14.	Low Low Low – Low Low Low	(S)			
15.	High High High – Low Low Low	(D)			
16.	Low High Low – Low High Low	(S)			
17.	High High Low – Low High High	(D)			
18.	Low High Low – Low High High	(D)			
19.	High High High – High High High	(S)			
20.	Low Low High – High Low Low	(D)			
			/20	/20	/20	/20
			%	%	%	%

Observations:

Task D: 4:4 Discrimination

Goal: The student will discriminate pitch patterns in quiet with 90% or greater accuracy.

You will hear two sound patterns. Tell me if the patterns are the same (S) or different (D).

			Dates				
1.	High Low High Low – High Low High Low	(S)					
2.	Low High Low High – Low Low High High	(D)					
3.	High High High High – High Low Low High	(D)					
4.	Low High High Low – Low High High Low	(S)					
5.	High Low Low Low – High High Low Low	(D)					
6.	Low High High High – Low High High High	(S)					
7.	High Low Low High – High Low Low High	(S)					
8.	Low High Low Low – Low Low Low High	(D)					
9.	High Low High Low – High Low Low Low	(D)					
10.	Low Low High High – Low Low High High	(S)					
11.	High Low Low Low – High Low Low Low	(S)					
12.	Low High High Low – Low High High Low	(S)					
13.	High High Low High – High High Low Low	(D)					
14.	Low Low Low Low – Low Low Low Low	(S)					
15.	High Low Low High – Low High High Low	(D)					
16.	Low High Low High – High Low High Low	(D)					
17.	High High High High – High High High High	(S)					
18.	High Low High Low – High Low High High	(D)					
19.	High High Low High – High High High High	(D)					
20.	Low Low High Low – High Low Low High	(D)					
			20	20	20	20	
			%	%	%	%	

Observations:

Task E: 5:5 Discrimination

Goal: The student will discriminate pitch patterns in quiet with 90% or greater accuracy.

You will hear two sound patterns. Tell me if the patterns are the same (S) or different (D).

			Dates				
1.	Low Low High Low Low – Low Low High Low Low	(S)					
2.	High Low Low High High – High Low Low High Low	(D)					
3.	High Low High Low High – High Low High Low High	(S)					
4.	High Low High High High – High Low High High High	(S)					
5.	High Low Low Low High – High Low High High Low	(D)					
6.	Low High Low High Low – Low High Low High Low	(S)					
7.	Low Low High Low Low – Low High High High Low	(D)					
8.	High High Low Low Low – Low High High Low Low	(D)					
9.	Low High High High Low – Low High High High Low	(S)					
10.	Low Low High Low Low – Low High High Low High	(D)					
11.	High Low High Low High – High Low Low High Low	(D)					
12.	Low High High High High – Low High High High High	(S)					
13.	High Low Low High High – High High Low Low High	(D)					
14.	Low Low High High Low – Low Low High High Low	(S)					
15.	High High Low High High – High Low High Low Low	(D)					
16.	High Low Low High High – High High High Low Low	(D)					
17.	Low High Low Low High – Low High Low Low High	(S)					
18.	Low Low Low Low High – Low Low High High High	(D)					
19.	High High Low High High – High High Low High High	(S)					
20.	Low High Low Low High – Low High High Low High	(D)					
				/20	/20	/20	/20
				%	%	%	%

Observations:

Task F: 1:1 Discrimination in Noise

Goal: The student will discriminate pitch matches in noise with 90% or greater accuracy.

You will hear two sounds and some noise. Tell me if the sounds are the same (S) or different (D).

	Dates				
1.	Low – Low (S)				
2.	High – High (S)				
3.	Low – High (D)				
4.	High – High (S)				
5.	High – Low (D)				
6.	Low – Low (S)				
7.	Low – High (D)				
8.	High – Low (D)				
9.	High – High (S)				
10.	Low – Low (S)				
11.	High – Low (D)				
12.	Low – Low (S)				
13.	High – High (S)				
14.	Low – High (D)				
15.	High – Low (D)				
16.	Low – Low (S)				
17.	High – High (S)				
18.	Low – High (D)				
19.	High – Low (D)				
20.	Low – Low (S)				
		20	20	20	20
		%	%	%	%

Observations:

Task G: 2:2 Discrimination in Noise

Goal: The student will discriminate pitch patterns in noise with 90% or greater accuracy.

You will hear two sound patterns and some noise. Tell me if the patterns are the same (S) or different (D).

	Dates				
1.	High High – High High (S)				
2.	Low High – High Low (D)				
3.	Low Low – Low Low (S)				
4.	Low High – Low High (S)				
5.	High Low – Low High (D)				
6.	Low Low – High High (D)				
7.	Low High – High Low (D)				
8.	Low Low – Low Low (S)				
9.	High Low – High Low (S)				
10.	High High – Low Low (D)				
11.	High Low – Low Low (D)				
12.	Low High – Low High (S)				
13.	High High – High Low (D)				
14.	High Low – High Low (S)				
15.	Low Low – Low High (D)				
16.	High High – High High (S)				
17.	Low High – Low Low (D)				
18.	High Low – Low High (D)				
19.	Low Low – Low Low (S)				
20.	High High – Low High (D)				
		20	20	20	20
		%	%	%	%

Observations:

Task H: 3:3 Discrimination in Noise

Goal: The student will discriminate pitch patterns in noise with 90% or greater accuracy.

You will hear two sound patterns and some noise. Tell me if the patterns are the same (S) or different (D).

		Dates				
1.	High Low High – High Low High	(S)				
2.	High Low High – High High Low	(D)				
3.	High Low Low – High Low Low	(S)				
4.	Low High Low – Low High Low	(S)				
5.	Low High Low – Low Low High	(D)				
6.	High Low Low – High High Low	(D)				
7.	Low High High – Low High Low	(D)				
8.	Low Low Low – Low Low Low	(S)				
9.	High Low High – High Low High	(S)				
10.	Low High High – Low Low Low	(D)				
11.	High Low High – Low High Low	(D)				
12.	High High Low – High High Low	(S)				
13.	Low High High – High Low High	(D)				
14.	High Low Low – High Low Low	(S)				
15.	High Low Low – Low High High	(D)				
16.	High High High – High High High	(S)				
17.	Low High High – Low Low High	(D)				
18.	Low High Low – Low Low Low	(D)				
19.	Low Low Low – Low Low Low	(S)				
20.	Low High High – Low High Low	(D)				
			20	20	20	20
			%	%	%	%

Observations:

Task 1: 4:4 Discrimination in Noise

Goal: The student will discriminate pitch patterns in noise with 90% or greater accuracy.

You will hear two sound patterns and some noise. Tell me if the patterns are the same (S) or different (D).

		Dates				
1.	High Low High Low – High Low High Low	(S)				
2.	Low Low Low High – Low Low Low High	(S)				
3.	High Low High High – High Low Low High	(D)				
4.	High Low High High – Low High Low High	(D)				
5.	Low High Low Low – High High Low Low	(D)				
6.	Low High High Low – Low High High Low	(S)				
7.	High High Low Low – High Low High High	(D)				
8.	Low Low Low Low – Low Low Low Low	(S)				
9.	Low High Low High – High Low Low Low	(D)				
10.	High Low Low High – Low High High Low	(D)				
11.	Low High Low Low – High Low High Low	(D)				
12.	Low High High High – Low High High High	(S)				
13.	High High Low Low – High High Low Low	(S)				
14.	High Low Low Low – High Low Low Low	(S)				
15.	High High High High – Low Low Low Low	(D)				
16.	High Low High Low – High Low High Low	(S)				
17.	Low High High Low – Low High Low High	(D)				
18.	Low High High Low – Low High High High	(D)				
19.	High High High High – High High High High	(S)				
20.	Low High Low High – High Low Low Low	(D)				
			/20	/20	/20	/20
			%	%	%	%

Observations:

Task J: 5:5 Discrimination in Noise

Goal: The student will discriminate pitch patterns in noise with 90% or greater accuracy.

You will hear two sound patterns and some noise. Tell me if the patterns are the same (S) or different (D).

		Dates				
1.	Low High Low High Low – Low High Low High Low	(S)				
2.	Low High Low Low High – Low Low High High High	(D)				
3.	Low High Low High Low – High Low Low High Low	(D)				
4.	High Low High High Low – High Low High High Low	(S)				
5.	Low High Low Low Low – High High Low Low Low	(D)				
6.	High Low High High High – High Low High High High	(S)				
7.	High High High Low High – High Low Low Low High	(D)				
8.	Low High Low Low High – High Low Low Low High	(D)				
9.	High Low Low Low Low – High Low Low Low Low	(S)				
10.	High Low Low High High – High Low Low High High	(S)				
11.	High Low High Low Low – High Low Low High Low	(D)				
12.	Low Low High High Low – High Low Low High High	(D)				
13.	High High Low Low High – High Low High Low High	(D)				
14.	High Low High Low High – High Low High Low High	(S)				
15.	High Low Low Low High – Low High High High Low	(D)				
16.	Low High Low High Low – High Low High Low Low	(D)				
17.	High High Low High High – High High Low High High	(S)				
18.	Low High Low High Low – High Low High High High	(D)				
19.	Low High High Low High – High High High Low High	(D)				
20.	Low High High High Low – Low High High High Low	(S)				
			20	20	20	20
			%	%	%	%

Observations:

Task K: Two-Unit Repetition

Goal: The student will repeat pitch patterns in quiet with 90% or greater accuracy.

You will hear a sound pattern. Repeat the pattern you hear.

Dates				
1. High Low				
2. Low High				
3. High High				
4. Low High				
5. Low Low				
6. High Low				
7. High High				
8. Low Low				
9. High Low				
10. Low High				
11. High Low				
12. High High				
13. Low High				
14. Low Low				
15. High High				
16. Low High				
17. High Low				
18. High High				
19. Low High				
20. High Low				
	20	20	20	20
	%	%	%	%

Observations:

Temporal Patterning
Copyright © 2007 LinguiSystems, Inc.

Unit One: Pitch Variation
Differential Processing Training Program: Acoustic Tasks

Task L: Three-Unit Repetition

Goal: The student will repeat pitch patterns in quiet with 90% or greater accuracy.

You will hear a sound pattern. Repeat the pattern you hear.

Dates				
1. Low High Low				
2. Low High High				
3. High High Low				
4. High Low Low				
5. Low Low High				
6. High High High				
7. Low High High				
8. High Low High				
9. Low Low Low				
10. Low High High				
11. High Low Low				
12. Low Low High				
13. High High High				
14. Low High High				
15. Low Low Low				
16. High Low High				
17. High High High				
18. High Low Low				
19. Low Low High				
20. Low Low Low				
	20	20	20	20
	%	%	%	%

Observations:

Task M: Four-Unit Repetition

Goal: The student will repeat pitch patterns in quiet with 90% or greater accuracy.

You will hear a sound pattern. Repeat the pattern you hear.

Dates				
1. High Low Low High				
2. Low High High High				
3. High Low High High				
4. Low Low Low High				
5. Low High High High				
6. Low Low Low Low				
7. High Low Low High				
8. High High Low High				
9. Low Low Low High				
10. High Low High Low				
11. High Low Low High				
12. High High Low Low				
13. Low High High High				
14. High Low Low High				
15. Low Low High High				
16. Low High High Low				
17. High Low High High				
18. Low Low Low High				
19. High High High High				
20. High Low Low Low				
	20	20	20	20
	%	%	%	%

Observations:

Task N: Five-Unit Repetition

Goal: The student will repeat pitch patterns in quiet with 90% or greater accuracy.

You will hear a sound pattern. Repeat the pattern you hear.

	Dates				
1.	High Low Low High Low				
2.	High High High High High				
3.	Low Low High Low High				
4.	High Low High High Low				
5.	Low Low High Low High				
6.	High Low High High Low				
7.	High Low High Low High				
8.	High High Low Low High				
9.	Low High Low Low High				
10.	Low High High Low High				
11.	High Low High Low Low				
12.	Low High High High Low				
13.	High High High Low Low				
14.	Low Low Low High Low				
15.	Low High Low High Low				
16.	High Low Low Low Low				
17.	Low High Low High High				
18.	High Low High High High				
19.	High High High Low High				
20.	Low Low Low Low High				
		20	20	20	20
		%	%	%	%

Observations:

Task O: Two-Unit Repetition in Noise

Goal: The student will repeat pitch patterns in noise with 90% or greater accuracy.

You will hear a sound pattern and some noise. Repeat the pattern you hear.

Dates				
1. High Low				
2. Low High				
3. Low Low				
4. Low High				
5. High High				
6. High Low				
7. Low High				
8. High Low				
9. Low Low				
10. High Low				
11. Low Low				
12. High Low				
13. High High				
14. High Low				
15. Low High				
16. High Low				
17. Low Low				
18. High High				
19. Low High				
20. Low Low				
	20	20	20	20
	%	%	%	%

Observations:

Task P: Three-Unit Repetition in Noise

Goal: The student will repeat pitch patterns in noise with 90% or greater accuracy.

You will hear a sound pattern and some noise. Repeat the pattern you hear.

Dates				
1. Low High Low				
2. Low Low Low				
3. Low High High				
4. High High Low				
5. Low Low High				
6. High Low High				
7. Low High High				
8. High High High				
9. High Low Low				
10. Low High High				
11. High Low Low				
12. Low Low High				
13. High High High				
14. High Low High				
15. Low Low Low				
16. Low High High				
17. High High High				
18. Low Low High				
19. High Low Low				
20. Low Low Low				
	20	20	20	20
	%	%	%	%

Observations:

Task Q: Four-Unit Repetition in Noise

Goal: The student will repeat pitch patterns in noise with 90% or greater accuracy.

You will hear a sound pattern and some noise. Repeat the pattern you hear.

	Dates				
1.	Low High High High				
2.	High Low Low High				
3.	High Low High High				
4.	Low Low Low Low				
5.	Low High High High				
6.	Low Low Low High				
7.	High High Low High				
8.	High Low Low High				
9.	Low Low Low High				
10.	High Low High Low				
11.	Low High High High				
12.	High High Low Low				
13.	High Low Low High				
14.	Low Low Low High				
15.	Low Low High High				
16.	High High High High				
17.	Low High High Low				
18.	High Low Low Low				
19.	High Low High High				
20.	Low High Low High				
		20	20	20	20
		%	%	%	%

Observations:

Temporal Patterning
Copyright © 2007 LinguiSystems, Inc.

Unit One: Pitch Variation
Differential Processing Training Program: Acoustic Tasks

Task R: Five-Unit Repetition in Noise

Goal: The student will repeat pitch patterns in noise with 90% or greater accuracy.

You will hear a sound pattern and some noise. Repeat the pattern you hear.

	Dates				
1.	High Low High High Low				
2.	Low High High High High				
3.	High Low Low High Low				
4.	Low Low High Low High				
5.	Low Low High Low High				
6.	High Low High Low High				
7.	High Low High High Low				
8.	High High Low Low High				
9.	Low High Low Low High				
10.	High Low High Low Low				
11.	High High High Low Low				
12.	Low High High Low High				
13.	Low High High High Low				
14.	High Low Low Low Low				
15.	Low Low Low High Low				
16.	Low High Low High Low				
17.	Low Low Low Low High				
18.	Low High Low High High				
19.	Low High High Low High				
20.	High Low High High High				
		20	20	20	20
		%	%	%	%

Observations:

Task A: 1:1 Discrimination

Goal: The student will discriminate loudness matches in quiet with 90% or greater accuracy.

You will hear two sounds. Tell me if the sounds are the same (S) or different (D).

	Dates				
1.	Soft – LOUD	(D)			
2.	LOUD – LOUD	(S)			
3.	Soft – Soft	(S)			
4.	LOUD – Soft	(D)			
5.	LOUD – LOUD	(S)			
6.	Soft – LOUD	(D)			
7.	Soft – Soft	(S)			
8.	LOUD – Soft	(D)			
9.	Soft – Soft	(S)			
10.	LOUD – LOUD	(S)			
11.	Soft – LOUD	(D)			
12.	LOUD – LOUD	(S)			
13.	LOUD – Soft	(D)			
14.	Soft – Soft	(S)			
15.	Soft – LOUD	(D)			
16.	LOUD – Soft	(D)			
17.	Soft – Soft	(S)			
18.	LOUD – Soft	(D)			
19.	LOUD – LOUD	(S)			
20.	LOUD – Soft	(D)			
			20	20	20	20
			%	%	%	%

Observations:

Temporal Patterning
Copyright © 2007 LinguiSystems, Inc.

Unit Two: Loudness Variation
Differential Processing Training Program: Acoustic Tasks

Task B: 2:2 Discrimination

Goal: The student will discriminate loudness patterns in quiet with 90% or greater accuracy.

You will hear two sound patterns. Tell me if the patterns are the same (S) or different (D).

		Dates				
1.	Soft Soft – Soft LOUD	(D)				
2.	Soft LOUD – Soft LOUD	(S)				
3.	LOUD Soft – LOUD LOUD	(D)				
4.	Soft Soft – Soft Soft	(S)				
5.	LOUD LOUD – Soft LOUD	(D)				
6.	Soft LOUD – LOUD LOUD	(D)				
7.	LOUD Soft – LOUD Soft	(S)				
8.	LOUD LOUD – LOUD LOUD	(S)				
9.	Soft LOUD – LOUD Soft	(D)				
10.	LOUD Soft – Soft Soft	(D)				
11.	LOUD LOUD – Soft LOUD	(D)				
12.	Soft Soft – Soft Soft	(S)				
13.	LOUD Soft – Soft Soft	(D)				
14.	LOUD LOUD – LOUD LOUD	(S)				
15.	Soft LOUD – Soft Soft	(D)				
16.	LOUD Soft – Soft Soft	(D)				
17.	LOUD Soft – LOUD Soft	(S)				
18.	Soft Soft – LOUD LOUD	(D)				
19.	LOUD Soft – LOUD LOUD	(D)				
20.	Soft LOUD – Soft LOUD	(S)				
			20	20	20	20
			%	%	%	%

Observations:

Task C: 3:3 Discrimination

Goal: The student will discriminate loudness patterns in quiet with 90% or greater accuracy.

You will hear two sound patterns. Tell me if the patterns are the same (S) or different (D).

			Dates				
1.	LOUD LOUD Soft – LOUD LOUD Soft	(S)					
2.	Soft LOUD Soft – Soft LOUD LOUD	(D)					
3.	Soft LOUD LOUD – LOUD Soft LOUD	(D)					
4.	LOUD Soft LOUD – LOUD Soft LOUD	(S)					
5.	Soft Soft LOUD – LOUD Soft Soft	(D)					
6.	Soft LOUD Soft – LOUD Soft Soft	(D)					
7.	LOUD LOUD LOUD – LOUD Soft Soft	(D)					
8.	Soft Soft Soft – Soft Soft Soft	(S)					
9.	LOUD Soft LOUD – Soft Soft LOUD	(D)					
10.	LOUD Soft Soft – LOUD Soft Soft	(S)					
11.	Soft LOUD Soft – Soft LOUD Soft	(S)					
12.	LOUD Soft LOUD – Soft Soft LOUD	(D)					
13.	Soft LOUD LOUD – Soft LOUD LOUD	(S)					
14.	LOUD LOUD LOUD – LOUD Soft LOUD	(D)					
15.	Soft Soft LOUD – Soft Soft LOUD	(S)					
16.	LOUD LOUD Soft – LOUD LOUD Soft	(S)					
17.	LOUD Soft Soft – LOUD LOUD Soft	(D)					
18.	Soft Soft Soft – LOUD LOUD LOUD	(D)					
19.	LOUD LOUD Soft – LOUD Soft LOUD	(D)					
20.	Soft LOUD Soft – Soft LOUD Soft	(S)					
			/20	/20	/20	/20	
			%	%	%	%	

Observations:

Task D: 4:4 Discrimination

Goal: The student will discriminate loudness patterns in quiet with 90% or greater accuracy.

You will hear two sound patterns. Tell me if the patterns are the same (S) or different (D).

			Dates				
1.	Soft Soft LOUD LOUD – Soft Soft LOUD LOUD	(S)					
2.	Soft LOUD Soft LOUD – Soft Soft LOUD Soft	(D)					
3.	LOUD LOUD Soft Soft – LOUD LOUD LOUD Soft	(D)					
4.	Soft LOUD LOUD Soft – Soft LOUD LOUD Soft	(S)					
5.	LOUD LOUD LOUD Soft – LOUD LOUD Soft Soft	(D)					
6.	LOUD Soft Soft LOUD – LOUD Soft Soft LOUD	(S)					
7.	LOUD Soft Soft Soft – LOUD LOUD Soft Soft	(D)					
8.	Soft Soft Soft LOUD – LOUD Soft Soft Soft	(D)					
9.	LOUD Soft LOUD Soft – LOUD LOUD LOUD LOUD	(D)					
10.	LOUD LOUD Soft Soft – LOUD LOUD Soft Soft	(S)					
11.	Soft LOUD Soft LOUD – Soft LOUD Soft LOUD	(S)					
12.	LOUD LOUD LOUD Soft – LOUD LOUD Soft LOUD	(D)					
13.	Soft Soft Soft Soft – Soft LOUD Soft Soft	(D)					
14.	LOUD Soft Soft LOUD – LOUD Soft Soft LOUD	(S)					
15.	LOUD Soft LOUD Soft–LOUD Soft LOUD Soft	(S)					
16.	LOUD Soft Soft Soft – LOUD Soft Soft LOUD	(D)					
17.	LOUD LOUD Soft LOUD – Soft LOUD Soft LOUD	(D)					
18.	Soft LOUD LOUD Soft – Soft Soft LOUD LOUD	(D)					
19.	Soft Soft Soft LOUD – Soft Soft Soft LOUD	(S)					
20.	LOUD LOUD Soft Soft – LOUD LOUD Soft Soft	(S)					
			/20	/20	/20	/20	
			%	%	%	%	

Observations:

Task E: 5:5 Discrimination

Goal: The student will discriminate loudness patterns in quiet with 90% or greater accuracy.

You will hear two sound patterns. Tell me if the patterns are the same (S) or different (D).

			Dates				
1.	Soft LOUD Soft LOUD Soft – Soft LOUD Soft LOUD Soft	(S)					
2.	LOUD Soft Soft LOUD Soft – LOUD LOUD LOUD Soft Soft	(D)					
3.	Soft LOUD LOUD LOUD Soft – Soft LOUD LOUD LOUD Soft	(S)					
4.	LOUD LOUD Soft Soft LOUD – LOUD LOUD Soft Soft LOUD	(S)					
5.	LOUD Soft Soft Soft LOUD – LOUD Soft Soft LOUD Soft	(D)					
6.	Soft Soft LOUD LOUD Soft – Soft LOUD Soft Soft LOUD	(D)					
7.	LOUD LOUD Soft LOUD LOUD – LOUD LOUD Soft LOUD LOUD	(S)					
8.	LOUD LOUD Soft Soft Soft – LOUD LOUD Soft LOUD LOUD	(D)					
9.	LOUD Soft LOUD LOUD LOUD – LOUD Soft LOUD LOUD LOUD	(S)					
10.	Soft LOUD Soft Soft LOUD – Soft LOUD LOUD LOUD Soft	(D)					
11.	LOUD Soft Soft Soft LOUD – LOUD Soft Soft Soft LOUD	(S)					
12.	Soft LOUD LOUD Soft LOUD – Soft LOUD Soft Soft Soft	(D)					
13.	LOUD LOUD LOUD LOUD Soft – Soft Soft Soft LOUD LOUD	(D)					
14.	Soft LOUD Soft Soft Soft – Soft LOUD Soft Soft Soft	(S)					
15.	LOUD Soft LOUD Soft Soft – LOUD LOUD LOUD Soft Soft	(D)					
16.	Soft LOUD LOUD LOUD LOUD – LOUD Soft Soft Soft LOUD	(D)					
17.	LOUD Soft Soft Soft Soft – LOUD Soft Soft Soft Soft	(S)					
18.	Soft Soft LOUD Soft LOUD – LOUD LOUD Soft Soft LOUD	(D)					
19.	Soft LOUD Soft LOUD LOUD – LOUD LOUD LOUD Soft LOUD	(D)					
20.	LOUD LOUD Soft Soft Soft – LOUD LOUD Soft Soft Soft	(S)					
				20	20	20	20
				%	%	%	%

Observations:

Task F: 1:1 Discrimination in Noise

Goal: The student will discriminate loudness matches in noise with 90% or greater accuracy.

You will hear two sounds and some noise. Tell me if the sounds are the same (S) or different (D).

	Dates				
1.	LOUD – LOUD (S)				
2.	LOUD – Soft (D)				
3.	Soft – Soft (S)				
4.	Soft – LOUD (D)				
5.	LOUD – LOUD (S)				
6.	Soft – Soft (S)				
7.	Soft – LOUD (D)				
8.	LOUD – Soft (D)				
9.	LOUD – LOUD (S)				
10.	Soft – Soft (S)				
11.	LOUD – Soft (D)				
12.	Soft – Soft (S)				
13.	Soft – LOUD (D)				
14.	LOUD – LOUD (S)				
15.	Soft – Soft (S)				
16.	Soft – LOUD (D)				
17.	LOUD – Soft (D)				
18.	Soft – Soft (S)				
19.	LOUD – Soft (D)				
20.	LOUD – LOUD (S)				
		20	20	20	20
		%	%	%	%

Observations:

Task G: 2:2 Discrimination in Noise

Goal: The student will discriminate loudness patterns in noise with 90% or greater accuracy.

You will hear two sound patterns and some noise. Tell me if the patterns are the same (S) or different (D).

		Dates				
1.	LOUD Soft – LOUD LOUD	(D)				
2.	Soft Soft – Soft LOUD	(D)				
3.	Soft LOUD – Soft LOUD	(S)				
4.	Soft Soft – Soft Soft	(S)				
5.	LOUD LOUD – Soft LOUD	(D)				
6.	LOUD LOUD – LOUD LOUD	(S)				
7.	LOUD Soft – LOUD Soft	(S)				
8.	LOUD LOUD – Soft LOUD	(D)				
9.	Soft LOUD – LOUD Soft	(D)				
10.	LOUD Soft – Soft Soft	(D)				
11.	Soft LOUD – LOUD LOUD	(D)				
12.	Soft Soft – Soft Soft	(S)				
13.	LOUD LOUD – LOUD LOUD	(S)				
14.	LOUD Soft – Soft Soft	(D)				
15.	LOUD Soft – LOUD Soft	(S)				
16.	LOUD Soft – Soft Soft	(D)				
17.	Soft LOUD – Soft Soft	(D)				
18.	Soft LOUD – Soft LOUD	(S)				
19.	LOUD Soft – LOUD LOUD	(D)				
20.	Soft Soft – LOUD LOUD	(D)				
			20	20	20	20
			%	%	%	%

Observations:

Temporal Patterning
Copyright © 2007 LinguiSystems, Inc.

Unit Two: Loudness Variation
Differential Processing Training Program: Acoustic Tasks

Task H: 3:3 Discrimination in Noise

Goal: The student will discriminate loudness patterns in noise with 90% or greater accuracy.

You will hear two sound patterns and some noise. Tell me if the patterns are the same (S) or different (D).

		Dates				
1.	LOUD Soft LOUD – LOUD Soft LOUD	(S)				
2.	Soft LOUD Soft – Soft LOUD LOUD	(D)				
3.	LOUD LOUD Soft – LOUD LOUD Soft	(S)				
4.	Soft LOUD LOUD – LOUD Soft LOUD	(D)				
5.	Soft Soft LOUD – LOUD Soft Soft	(D)				
6.	LOUD LOUD LOUD – LOUD Soft Soft	(D)				
7.	Soft LOUD Soft – LOUD Soft Soft	(D)				
8.	Soft Soft Soft – Soft Soft Soft	(S)				
9.	LOUD Soft LOUD – Soft Soft LOUD	(D)				
10.	LOUD Soft Soft – LOUD Soft Soft	(S)				
11.	LOUD Soft LOUD – Soft Soft LOUD	(D)				
12.	Soft Soft LOUD – Soft Soft LOUD	(S)				
13.	Soft LOUD LOUD – Soft LOUD LOUD	(S)				
14.	LOUD LOUD LOUD – LOUD Soft LOUD	(D)				
15.	Soft LOUD Soft – Soft LOUD Soft	(S)				
16.	LOUD Soft Soft – LOUD LOUD Soft	(D)				
17.	LOUD LOUD Soft – LOUD LOUD Soft	(S)				
18.	Soft Soft Soft – LOUD LOUD LOUD	(D)				
19.	Soft LOUD Soft – Soft LOUD Soft	(S)				
20.	LOUD LOUD Soft – LOUD Soft LOUD	(D)				
			20	20	20	20
			%	%	%	%

Observations:

Task I: 4:4 Discrimination in Noise

Goal: The student will discriminate loudness patterns in noise with 90% or greater accuracy.

You will hear two sound patterns and some noise. Tell me if the patterns are the same (S) or different (D).

		Dates				
1.	LOUD LOUD Soft Soft – LOUD LOUD LOUD Soft	(D)				
2.	Soft LOUD Soft LOUD – Soft Soft LOUD Soft	(D)				
3.	Soft Soft LOUD LOUD – Soft Soft LOUD LOUD	(S)				
4.	LOUD Soft LOUD Soft – LOUD LOUD LOUD LOUD	(D)				
5.	LOUD LOUD LOUD Soft – LOUD LOUD Soft Soft	(D)				
6.	LOUD Soft Soft LOUD – LOUD Soft Soft LOUD	(S)				
7.	Soft Soft Soft LOUD – LOUD Soft Soft Soft	(D)				
8.	LOUD Soft Soft Soft – LOUD LOUD Soft Soft	(D)				
9.	Soft LOUD LOUD Soft – Soft LOUD LOUD Soft	(S)				
10.	Soft Soft Soft Soft – Soft LOUD Soft Soft	(D)				
11.	Soft LOUD Soft LOUD – Soft LOUD Soft LOUD	(S)				
12.	Soft LOUD LOUD Soft – Soft LOUD Soft LOUD	(D)				
13.	Soft LOUD Soft LOUD – Soft LOUD Soft LOUD	(S)				
14.	LOUD Soft Soft LOUD – LOUD Soft Soft LOUD	(S)				
15.	LOUD Soft Soft Soft – LOUD Soft Soft LOUD	(D)				
16.	LOUD LOUD Soft Soft – LOUD LOUD Soft Soft	(S)				
17.	LOUD LOUD Soft LOUD – Soft LOUD Soft LOUD	(D)				
18.	LOUD LOUD Soft Soft – LOUD LOUD Soft Soft	(S)				
19.	Soft Soft Soft LOUD – Soft Soft Soft LOUD	(S)				
20.	Soft LOUD LOUD Soft – Soft Soft LOUD LOUD	(D)				
			20	20	20	20
			%	%	%	%

Observations:

Temporal Patterning
Copyright © 2007 LinguiSystems, Inc.
Unit Two: Loudness Variation
Differential Processing Training Program: Acoustic Tasks

Task J: 5:5 Discrimination in Noise

Goal: The student will discriminate loudness patterns in noise with 90% or greater accuracy.

You will hear two sound patterns and some noise. Tell me if the patterns are the same (S) or different (D).

		Dates				
1.	LOUD LOUD Soft LOUD LOUD – LOUD LOUD Soft LOUD LOUD	(S)				
2.	LOUD Soft Soft LOUD Soft – LOUD LOUD LOUD Soft Soft	(D)				
3.	Soft LOUD LOUD LOUD Soft – Soft LOUD LOUD LOUD Soft	(S)				
4.	Soft LOUD Soft LOUD Soft – Soft LOUD Soft LOUD Soft	(S)				
5.	LOUD LOUD Soft Soft LOUD – LOUD LOUD Soft Soft LOUD	(S)				
6.	Soft Soft LOUD LOUD Soft – Soft LOUD Soft Soft LOUD	(D)				
7.	LOUD Soft Soft Soft LOUD – LOUD Soft Soft LOUD Soft	(D)				
8.	LOUD LOUD Soft Soft Soft – LOUD LOUD Soft LOUD LOUD	(D)				
9.	LOUD Soft Soft Soft LOUD – LOUD Soft Soft Soft LOUD	(S)				
10.	LOUD Soft LOUD LOUD LOUD – LOUD Soft LOUD LOUD LOUD	(S)				
11.	Soft LOUD Soft Soft LOUD – Soft LOUD LOUD LOUD Soft	(D)				
12.	Soft LOUD Soft Soft Soft – Soft LOUD Soft Soft Soft	(S)				
13.	LOUD LOUD LOUD LOUD Soft – Soft Soft Soft LOUD LOUD	(D)				
14.	Soft LOUD LOUD Soft LOUD – Soft LOUD Soft Soft Soft	(D)				
15.	Soft LOUD LOUD LOUD LOUD – LOUD Soft Soft Soft LOUD	(D)				
16.	LOUD Soft LOUD Soft Soft – LOUD LOUD LOUD Soft Soft	(D)				
17.	LOUD Soft Soft Soft Soft – LOUD Soft Soft Soft Soft	(S)				
18.	LOUD LOUD Soft Soft Soft – LOUD LOUD Soft Soft Soft	(S)				
19.	Soft LOUD Soft LOUD Soft – LOUD LOUD LOUD Soft Soft	(D)				
20.	Soft Soft LOUD Soft LOUD – LOUD LOUD Soft Soft LOUD	(D)				
			20	20	20	20
			%	%	%	%

Observations:

Task K: Two-Unit Repetition

Goal: The student will repeat loudness patterns in quiet with 90% or greater accuracy.

You will hear a sound pattern. Repeat the pattern you hear.

Dates				
1. Soft LOUD				
2. LOUD Soft				
3. Soft LOUD				
4. LOUD LOUD				
5. LOUD Soft				
6. Soft LOUD				
7. Soft Soft				
8. LOUD Soft				
9. LOUD LOUD				
10. Soft Soft				
11. LOUD Soft				
12. Soft Soft				
13. LOUD LOUD				
14. LOUD Soft				
15. LOUD LOUD				
16. Soft LOUD				
17. Soft Soft				
18. LOUD Soft				
19. LOUD LOUD				
20. Soft LOUD				
	20	20	20	20
	%	%	%	%

Observations:

Temporal Patterning
Copyright © 2007 LinguiSystems, Inc.

Unit Two: Loudness Variation
Differential Processing Training Program: Acoustic Tasks

Task L: Three-Unit Repetition

Goal: The student will repeat loudness patterns in quiet with 90% or greater accuracy.

You will hear a sound pattern. Repeat the pattern you hear.

	Dates				
1.	LOUD Soft LOUD				
2.	Soft LOUD Soft				
3.	Soft LOUD LOUD				
4.	Soft LOUD Soft				
5.	LOUD LOUD Soft				
6.	LOUD Soft Soft				
7.	Soft Soft Soft				
8.	LOUD Soft LOUD				
9.	LOUD Soft Soft				
10.	LOUD LOUD LOUD				
11.	Soft Soft LOUD				
12.	LOUD LOUD Soft				
13.	Soft Soft Soft				
14.	LOUD Soft Soft				
15.	Soft LOUD Soft				
16.	LOUD Soft Soft				
17.	LOUD Soft LOUD				
18.	Soft LOUD LOUD				
19.	Soft Soft LOUD				
20.	LOUD LOUD Soft				
		20	20	20	20
		%	%	%	%

Observations:

Task M: Four-Unit Repetition

Goal: The student will repeat loudness patterns in quiet with 90% or greater accuracy.

You will hear a sound pattern. Repeat the pattern you hear.

Dates				
1. LOUD Soft LOUD Soft				
2. LOUD Soft Soft LOUD				
3. Soft LOUD LOUD LOUD				
4. Soft Soft LOUD LOUD				
5. LOUD Soft LOUD LOUD				
6. LOUD LOUD Soft LOUD				
7. Soft LOUD LOUD Soft				
8. Soft Soft LOUD Soft				
9. Soft Soft Soft LOUD				
10. LOUD Soft LOUD LOUD				
11. LOUD Soft Soft Soft				
12. Soft Soft Soft Soft				
13. LOUD Soft LOUD Soft				
14. LOUD LOUD Soft LOUD				
15. Soft LOUD Soft Soft				
16. LOUD LOUD LOUD LOUD				
17. LOUD Soft Soft LOUD				
18. Soft Soft LOUD Soft				
19. Soft LOUD LOUD Soft				
20. Soft Soft Soft LOUD				
	/20	/20	/20	/20
	%	%	%	%

Observations:

Task N: Five-Unit Repetition

Goal: The student will repeat loudness patterns in quiet with 90% or greater accuracy.

You will hear a sound pattern. Repeat the pattern you hear.

	Dates				
1.	LOUD Soft Soft LOUD LOUD				
2.	Soft Soft LOUD LOUD LOUD				
3.	Soft LOUD Soft LOUD LOUD				
4.	Soft Soft LOUD Soft Soft				
5.	LOUD Soft LOUD Soft Soft				
6.	LOUD LOUD Soft LOUD Soft				
7.	Soft LOUD LOUD LOUD Soft				
8.	Soft Soft Soft LOUD Soft				
9.	LOUD LOUD Soft Soft Soft				
10.	Soft Soft Soft Soft LOUD				
11.	LOUD Soft Soft LOUD LOUD				
12.	Soft LOUD LOUD Soft LOUD				
13.	LOUD Soft Soft Soft LOUD				
14.	LOUD LOUD Soft Soft Soft				
15.	Soft LOUD Soft Soft LOUD				
16.	Soft LOUD LOUD Soft LOUD				
17.	LOUD Soft LOUD LOUD LOUD				
18.	LOUD LOUD Soft LOUD Soft				
19.	Soft LOUD Soft Soft Soft				
20.	LOUD Soft Soft Soft Soft				
		20	20	20	20
		%	%	%	%

Observations:

Task O: Two-Unit Repetition in Noise

Goal: The student will repeat loudness patterns in noise with 90% or greater accuracy.

You will hear a sound pattern and some noise. Repeat the pattern you hear.

Dates				
1. Soft LOUD				
2. LOUD LOUD				
3. Soft LOUD				
4. LOUD Soft				
5. Soft Soft				
6. Soft LOUD				
7. LOUD Soft				
8. Soft Soft				
9. LOUD Soft				
10. LOUD LOUD				
11. Soft LOUD				
12. LOUD Soft				
13. LOUD LOUD				
14. Soft Soft				
15. LOUD Soft				
16. Soft Soft				
17. Soft LOUD				
18. LOUD LOUD				
19. Soft Soft				
20. Soft LOUD				
	20	20	20	20
	%	%	%	%

Observations:

Task P: Three-Unit Repetition in Noise

Goal: The student will repeat loudness patterns in noise with 90% or greater accuracy.

You will hear a sound pattern and some noise. Repeat the pattern you hear.

	Dates				
1.	Soft LOUD Soft				
2.	Soft LOUD LOUD				
3.	LOUD Soft LOUD				
4.	Soft Soft LOUD				
5.	LOUD LOUD Soft				
6.	Soft Soft Soft				
7.	LOUD Soft LOUD				
8.	LOUD Soft Soft				
9.	LOUD LOUD LOUD				
10.	LOUD Soft Soft				
11.	Soft Soft LOUD				
12.	Soft Soft Soft				
13.	LOUD LOUD Soft				
14.	LOUD Soft Soft				
15.	Soft LOUD Soft				
16.	LOUD Soft Soft				
17.	LOUD LOUD Soft				
18.	Soft LOUD LOUD				
19.	LOUD Soft LOUD				
20.	Soft Soft LOUD				
		20	20	20	20
		%	%	%	%

Observations:

Task Q: Four-Unit Repetition in Noise

Goal: The student will repeat loudness patterns in noise with 90% or greater accuracy.

You will hear a sound pattern and some noise. Repeat the pattern you hear.

	Dates				
1.	Soft Soft LOUD LOUD				
2.	LOUD Soft LOUD Soft				
3.	Soft LOUD LOUD LOUD				
4.	LOUD Soft Soft LOUD				
5.	LOUD Soft LOUD LOUD				
6.	Soft Soft LOUD Soft				
7.	Soft LOUD LOUD Soft				
8.	Soft Soft Soft LOUD				
9.	LOUD LOUD Soft LOUD				
10.	LOUD Soft Soft Soft				
11.	LOUD Soft LOUD LOUD				
12.	Soft Soft Soft Soft				
13.	LOUD Soft LOUD Soft				
14.	Soft LOUD Soft Soft				
15.	Soft Soft Soft LOUD				
16.	LOUD Soft Soft LOUD				
17.	LOUD LOUD LOUD LOUD				
18.	Soft Soft LOUD Soft				
19.	Soft LOUD LOUD Soft				
20.	LOUD LOUD Soft LOUD				
		20	20	20	20
		%	%	%	%

Observations:

Temporal Patterning
Copyright © 2007 LinguiSystems, Inc.

Unit Two: Loudness Variation
Differential Processing Training Program: Acoustic Tasks

Task R: Five-Unit Repetition in Noise

Goal: The student will repeat loudness patterns in noise with 90% or greater accuracy.

You will hear a sound pattern and some noise. Repeat the pattern you hear.

	Dates				
1.	Soft Soft LOUD Soft Soft				
2.	LOUD Soft Soft LOUD LOUD				
3.	LOUD LOUD Soft Soft Soft				
4.	Soft Soft LOUD LOUD LOUD				
5.	Soft LOUD Soft LOUD LOUD				
6.	LOUD Soft LOUD Soft Soft				
7.	Soft Soft Soft LOUD Soft				
8.	LOUD LOUD Soft LOUD Soft				
9.	Soft LOUD LOUD LOUD Soft				
10.	Soft Soft Soft Soft LOUD				
11.	LOUD Soft Soft LOUD LOUD				
12.	Soft LOUD LOUD Soft LOUD				
13.	Soft LOUD Soft Soft LOUD				
14.	LOUD LOUD Soft Soft Soft				
15.	LOUD Soft Soft Soft LOUD				
16.	Soft LOUD LOUD Soft LOUD				
17.	LOUD LOUD Soft LOUD Soft				
18.	LOUD Soft LOUD LOUD LOUD				
19.	Soft LOUD Soft Soft Soft				
20.	LOUD Soft Soft Soft LOUD				
		20	20	20	20
		%	%	%	%

Observations:

Task A: 1:1 Discrimination

Goal: The student will discriminate duration matches in quiet with 90% or greater accuracy.

You will hear two sounds. Tell me if the sounds are the same (S) or different (D).

	Dates				
1.	Short – Short (S)				
2.	Short – Long (D)				
3.	Long – Short (D)				
4.	Short – Long (D)				
5.	Long – Long (S)				
6.	Short – Short (S)				
7.	Short – Long (D)				
8.	Short – Short (S)				
9.	Long – Short (D)				
10.	Short – Long (D)				
11.	Long – Long (S)				
12.	Long – Short (D)				
13.	Short – Long (D)				
14.	Long – Short (D)				
15.	Long – Long (S)				
16.	Short – Long (D)				
17.	Short – Short (S)				
18.	Long – Short (D)				
19.	Short – Short (S)				
20.	Long – Short (D)				
		20	20	20	20
		%	%	%	%

Observations:

Task B: 2:2 Discrimination

Goal: The student will discriminate duration patterns in quiet with **90% or greater accuracy.**

You will hear two sound patterns. Tell me if the patterns are the same (S) or different (D).

		Dates				
1.	Short Long – Short Long	(S)				
2.	Long Long – Short Long	(D)				
3.	Long Short – Long Short	(S)				
4.	Long Long – Long Long	(S)				
5.	Short Short – Short Long	(D)				
6.	Long Short – Short Long	(D)				
7.	Short Short – Short Short	(S)				
8.	Long Short – Long Short	(S)				
9.	Short Short – Long Long	(D)				
10.	Short Long – Short Short	(D)				
11.	Long Long – Long Short	(D)				
12.	Short Long – Short Long	(S)				
13.	Short Short – Short Short	(S)				
14.	Long Short – Short Long	(D)				
15.	Long Long – Short Long	(D)				
16.	Short Short – Long Short	(D)				
17.	Long Short – Long Short	(S)				
18.	Long Long – Long Long	(S)				
19.	Short Long – Short Long	(S)				
20.	Long Short – Long Long	(D)				
			20	20	20	20
			%	%	%	%

Observations:

Task C: 3:3 Discrimination

Goal: The student will discriminate duration patterns in quiet with 90% or greater accuracy.

You will hear two sound patterns. Tell me if the patterns are the same (S) or different (D).

		Dates				
1.	Short Long Short – Short Long Short	(S)				
2.	Long Short Short – Long Short Short	(S)				
3.	Long Long Short – Long Short Short	(D)				
4.	Short Long Long – Long Short Long	(D)				
5.	Long Long Short – Long Long Short	(S)				
6.	Long Short Short – Long Short Long	(D)				
7.	Short Short Long – Short Short Long	(S)				
8.	Long Short Short – Short Short Long	(D)				
9.	Long Long Short – Long Short Short	(D)				
10.	Short Short Short – Long Long Long	(D)				
11.	Short Long Long – Short Long Long	(S)				
12.	Long Short Short – Long Long Short	(D)				
13.	Short Short Short – Long Short Short	(D)				
14.	Long Long Long – Long Long Long	(S)				
15.	Long Short Long – Long Long Short	(D)				
16.	Short Long Short – Short Long Short	(S)				
17.	Long Long Short – Long Long Short	(S)				
18.	Long Short Short – Short Short Short	(D)				
19.	Short Short Long – Long Short Short	(D)				
20.	Long Short Long – Long Short Long	(S)				
			20	20	20	20
			%	%	%	%

Observations:

Task D: 4:4 Discrimination

Goal: The student will discriminate duration patterns in quiet with 90% or greater accuracy.

You will hear two sound patterns. Tell me if the patterns are the same (S) or different (D).

			Dates				
1.	Short Long Short Long – Short Long Short Long	(S)					
2.	Short Long Long Short – Short Long Long Short	(S)					
3.	Long Short Long Short – Long Short Short Short	(D)					
4.	Long Short Long Long – Long Short Long Long	(S)					
5.	Short Short Long Long – Long Long Long Short	(D)					
6.	Long Short Long Long – Long Short Short Long	(D)					
7.	Short Long Short Long – Short Long Short Long	(S)					
8.	Short Short Short Long – Short Long Short Short	(D)					
9.	Long Long Short Long – Long Long Short Long	(S)					
10.	Short Long Short Long – Short Long Short Short	(D)					
11.	Long Long Long Short – Long Long Long Short	(S)					
12.	Short Long Long Long – Short Long Long Long	(S)					
13.	Long Short Short Long – Long Long Long Long	(D)					
14.	Long Short Long Short – Long Short Long Short	(S)					
15.	Short Long Long Short – Long Long Short Long	(D)					
16.	Long Long Long Long – Long Long Long Long	(S)					
17.	Short Long Short Short – Short Short Long Short	(D)					
18.	Long Long Long Short – Short Long Long Long	(D)					
19.	Short Long Long Short – Short Long Long Short	(S)					
20.	Short Short Short Short – Short Short Short Long	(D)					
			20	20	20	20	
			%	%	%	%	

Observations:

Task E: 5:5 Discrimination

Goal: The student will discriminate duration patterns in quiet with 90% or greater accuracy.

You will hear two sound patterns. Tell me if the patterns are the same (S) or different (D).

			Dates				
1.	Short Short Long Long Long – Short Short Long Long Long	(S)					
2.	Long Long Long Short Short – Long Long Long Short Long	(D)					
3.	Short Long Short Short Long – Short Long Short Short Long	(S)					
4.	Short Long Short Long Long – Short Long Short Long Long	(S)					
5.	Long Long Short Long Long – Long Long Long Short Short	(D)					
6.	Long Short Short Short Long – Long Short Short Short Long	(S)					
7.	Long Short Long Long Short – Short Long Short Short Short	(D)					
8.	Short Long Short Short Long – Short Long Long Short Short	(D)					
9.	Short Long Short Long Long – Short Long Short Long Long	(S)					
10.	Long Short Short Long Long – Long Short Long Long Long	(D)					
11.	Long Long Long Short Long – Long Long Long Short Long	(S)					
12.	Short Short Long Long Long – Short Short Long Long Long	(S)					
13.	Long Short Long Short Long – Long Short Long Short Short	(D)					
14.	Short Long Short Long Short – Short Long Short Long Short	(S)					
15.	Short Short Long Long Short – Long Long Short Short Long	(D)					
16.	Short Long Long Long Long – Short Long Long Long Long	(S)					
17.	Long Short Short Short Short – Short Short Short Short Long	(D)					
18.	Short Long Long Long Short – Short Long Short Long Long	(D)					
19.	Short Long Long Short Short – Short Long Long Short Short	(S)					
20.	Long Short Long Short Short – Short Short Long Long Short	(D)					
			20	20	20	20	
			%	%	%	%	

Observations:

Task F: 1:1 Discrimination in Noise

Goal: The student will discriminate duration matches in noise with 90% or greater accuracy.

You will hear two sounds and some noise. Tell me if the sounds are the same (S) or different (D).

	Dates				
1.	Long – Long	(S)				
2.	Long – Short	(D)				
3.	Short – Long	(D)				
4.	Long – Short	(D)				
5.	Short – Short	(S)				
6.	Short – Long	(D)				
7.	Long – Short	(D)				
8.	Short – Short	(S)				
9.	Long – Long	(S)				
10.	Short – Long	(D)				
11.	Long – Long	(S)				
12.	Long – Short	(D)				
13.	Short – Long	(D)				
14.	Short – Short	(S)				
15.	Long – Long	(S)				
16.	Short – Long	(D)				
17.	Short – Short	(S)				
18.	Long – Short	(D)				
19.	Long – Long	(S)				
20.	Long – Short	(D)				
			20	20	20	20
			%	%	%	%

Observations:

Task G: 2:2 Discrimination in Noise

Goal: The student will discriminate duration patterns in noise with 90% or greater accuracy.

You will hear two sound patterns and some noise. Tell me if the patterns are the same (S) or different (D).

	Dates				
1.	Long Short – Long Short (S)				
2.	Long Short – Short Long (D)				
3.	Short Long – Short Long (S)				
4.	Long Long – Long Long (S)				
5.	Long Short – Short Long (D)				
6.	Short Short – Short Long (D)				
7.	Short Long – Short Short (D)				
8.	Long Short – Long Short (S)				
9.	Short Short – Long Long (D)				
10.	Long Long – Long Short (D)				
11.	Short Long – Short Short (D)				
12.	Short Long – Short Long (S)				
13.	Long Short – Short Long (D)				
14.	Short Short – Short Short (S)				
15.	Long Long – Short Long (D)				
16.	Short Long – Long Short (D)				
17.	Long Short – Long Short (S)				
18.	Short Short – Short Short (S)				
19.	Short Long – Short Long (S)				
20.	Long Long – Short Long (D)				
		20	20	20	20
		%	%	%	%

Observations:

Task H: 3:3 Discrimination in Noise

Goal: The student will discriminate duration patterns in noise with 90% or greater accuracy.

You will hear two sound patterns and some noise. Tell me if the patterns are the same (S) or different (D).

		Dates				
1.	Long Short Long – Long Short Long	(S)				
2.	Short Long Short – Short Long Short	(S)				
3.	Short Long Short – Long Short Short	(D)				
4.	Short Long Long – Long Short Long	(D)				
5.	Long Long Short – Long Long Short	(S)				
6.	Long Long Short – Long Short Long	(D)				
7.	Long Short Short – Short Short Long	(D)				
8.	Short Short Long – Short Short Long	(S)				
9.	Long Long Short – Long Short Short	(D)				
10.	Short Short Short – Long Long Long	(D)				
11.	Short Long Long – Short Long Long	(S)				
12.	Long Short Short – Long Long Short	(D)				
13.	Short Short Long – Long Short Short	(D)				
14.	Short Long Short – Short Long Short	(S)				
15.	Long Short Long – Long Long Short	(D)				
16.	Long Long Long – Long Long Long	(S)				
17.	Short Short Long – Long Short Short	(D)				
18.	Long Short Short – Short Short Long	(D)				
19.	Long Long Short – Long Long Short	(S)				
20.	Long Short Long – Long Short Long	(S)				
			20	20	20	20
			%	%	%	%

Observations:

Task I: 4:4 Discrimination in Noise

Goal: The student will discriminate duration patterns in noise with 90% or greater accuracy.

You will hear two sound patterns and some noise. Tell me if the patterns are the same (S) or different (D).

		Dates				
1.	Long Short Long Long – Long Short Long Long	(S)				
2.	Short Long Short Long – Short Long Short Long	(S)				
3.	Long Short Long Short – Long Short Short Short	(D)				
4.	Short Short Long Long – Long Long Long Short	(D)				
5.	Short Long Long Short – Short Long Long Short	(S)				
6.	Short Long Short Long – Short Long Short Long	(S)				
7.	Long Short Long Long – Long Short Short Long	(D)				
8.	Short Short Short Long – Short Long Short Short	(D)				
9.	Long Long Short Long – Long Long Short Long	(S)				
10.	Long Long Long Short – Long Long Long Short	(S)				
11.	Short Long Short Long – Short Long Short Short	(D)				
12.	Short Long Long Long – Short Long Long Long	(S)				
13.	Long Short Short Long – Long Long Long Long	(D)				
14.	Short Long Long Short – Long Long Short Long	(D)				
15.	Long Short Long Short – Long Short Long Short	(S)				
16.	Long Long Long Long – Long Long Long Long	(S)				
17.	Short Long Short Short – Short Short Long Short	(D)				
18.	Short Short Short Short – Short Short Short Long	(D)				
19.	Long Long Long Short – Short Long Long Long	(D)				
20.	Short Long Long Short – Short Long Long Short	(S)				
			20	20	20	20
			%	%	%	%

Observations:

Task J: 5:5 Discrimination in Noise

Goal: The student will discriminate duration patterns in noise with 90% or greater accuracy.

You will hear two sound patterns and some noise. Tell me if the patterns are the same (S) or different (D).

			Dates				
1.	Short Long Short Short Long – Short Long Short Short Long	(S)					
2.	Long Short Long Short Short – Long Long Long Short Short	(D)					
3.	Short Short Long Long Long – Short Short Long Long Long	(S)					
4.	Short Long Short Long Long – Long Long Long Short Short	(D)					
5.	Long Long Short Long Long – Long Long Short Long Long	(S)					
6.	Long Short Short Short Long – Long Short Long Short Long	(D)					
7.	Long Long Long Short Long – Long Long Long Short Long	(S)					
8.	Short Long Short Short Long – Short Long Long Short Short	(D)					
9.	Long Long Short Long Long – Long Long Short Long Long	(S)					
10.	Long Short Short Long Long – Long Short Long Long Long	(D)					
11.	Long Short Long Long Short – Short Long Short Short Short	(D)					
12.	Short Short Long Long Long – Short Short Long Long Long	(S)					
13.	Long Short Long Short Long – Long Short Long Short Short	(D)					
14.	Short Long Short Long Short – Short Long Short Long Short	(S)					
15.	Long Short Long Long Short – Long Long Short Short Long	(D)					
16.	Short Long Long Long Long – Short Long Long Long Long	(S)					
17.	Short Short Short Short Short – Short Short Short Short Long	(D)					
18.	Long Long Short Long Short – Long Long Short Long Short	(S)					
19.	Short Long Long Short Short – Short Long Long Short Short	(S)					
20.	Long Short Long Short Long – Short Short Long Long Short	(D)					
			20	20	20	20	
			%	%	%	%	

Observations:

Task K: Two-Unit Repetition

Goal: The student will repeat duration patterns in quiet with 90% or greater accuracy.

You will hear a sound pattern. Repeat the pattern you hear.

Dates				
1. Long Short				
2. Long Long				
3. Short Long				
4. Short Long				
5. Long Short				
6. Short Short				
7. Short Long				
8. Long Short				
9. Short Short				
10. Short Long				
11. Long Long				
12. Short Long				
13. Long Short				
14. Long Long				
15. Short Short				
16. Long Short				
17. Long Long				
18. Short Long				
19. Short Short				
20. Long Short				
	20	20	20	20
	%	%	%	%

Observations:

Task L: Three-Unit Repetition

Goal: The student will repeat duration patterns in quiet with 90% or greater accuracy.

You will hear a sound pattern. Repeat the pattern you hear.

Dates				
1. Short Long Short				
2. Short Short Short				
3. Long Short Long				
4. Long Long Short				
5. Long Short Short				
6. Long Long Long				
7. Short Long Long				
8. Long Long Short				
9. Short Short Short				
10. Long Short Short				
11. Long Long Long				
12. Short Long Short				
13. Long Long Long				
14. Short Long Long				
15. Short Short Short				
16. Long Short Short				
17. Short Long Long				
18. Long Long Short				
19. Long Short Long				
20. Short Short Long				
	20	20	20	20
	%	%	%	%

Observations:

Task M: Four-Unit Repetition

Goal: The student will repeat duration patterns in quiet with **90% or greater accuracy.**

You will hear a sound pattern. Repeat the pattern you hear.

Dates				
1. Long Long Short Short				
2. Long Short Short Long				
3. Short Long Long Short				
4. Short Short Short Long				
5. Long Long Long Short				
6. Long Short Short Short				
7. Short Long Short Long				
8. Short Long Short Short				
9. Long Long Long Long				
10. Long Short Short Long				
11. Short Short Long Short				
12. Long Short Short Long				
13. Long Short Long Short				
14. Long Short Long Long				
15. Short Short Long Long				
16. Short Short Short Long				
17. Long Short Short Short				
18. Long Short Short Long				
19. Short Short Short Short				
20. Short Long Short Short				
	20	20	20	20
	%	%	%	%

Observations:

Task N: Five-Unit Repetition

Goal: The student will repeat duration patterns in quiet with 90% or greater accuracy.

You will hear a sound pattern. Repeat the pattern you hear.

	Dates				
1.	Long Short Long Long Short				
2.	Short Short Long Long Long				
3.	Long Short Long Short Long				
4.	Short Long Short Long Long				
5.	Short Short Short Short Long				
6.	Long Short Long Long Short				
7.	Short Short Short Long Long				
8.	Long Long Long Short Long				
9.	Long Short Long Short Long				
10.	Short Long Short Long Long				
11.	Short Long Long Long Short				
12.	Long Long Short Short Long				
13.	Long Short Long Long Short				
14.	Short Long Long Short Short				
15.	Long Short Short Short Long				
16.	Long Short Long Long Long				
17.	Short Long Short Short Short				
18.	Short Short Long Long Short				
19.	Long Short Short Short Short				
20.	Long Long Short Short Long				
		20	20	20	20
		%	%	%	%

Observations:

Task O: Two-Unit Repetition in Noise

Goal: The student will repeat duration patterns in noise with 90% or greater accuracy.

You will hear a sound pattern and some noise. Repeat the pattern you hear.

Dates				
1. Short Long				
2. Long Long				
3. Long Short				
4. Short Long				
5. Short Short				
6. Long Short				
7. Short Long				
8. Long Short				
9. Short Short				
10. Short Long				
11. Long Long				
12. Short Long				
13. Short Short				
14. Long Short				
15. Long Short				
16. Short Short				
17. Long Short				
18. Short Long				
19. Long Short				
20. Short Short				
	20	20	20	20
	%	%	%	%

Observations:

Task P: Three-Unit Repetition in Noise

Goal: The student will repeat duration patterns in noise with 90% or greater accuracy.

You will hear a sound pattern and some noise. Repeat the pattern you hear.

Dates				
1. Long Long Short				
2. Short Long Short				
3. Long Short Long				
4. Long Short Short				
5. Long Long Short				
6. Long Long Long				
7. Short Short Short				
8. Long Long Short				
9. Short Long Long				
10. Long Short Short				
11. Long Long Long				
12. Short Long Short				
13. Long Long Long				
14. Short Short Short				
15. Short Long Long				
16. Long Short Short				
17. Short Long Long				
18. Long Short Long				
19. Long Long Short				
20. Short Short Long				
	20 %	20 %	20 %	20 %

Observations:

Task Q: Four-Unit Repetition in Noise

Goal: The student will repeat duration patterns in noise with 90% or greater accuracy.

You will hear a sound pattern and some noise. Repeat the pattern you hear.

Dates				
1. Short Long Short Short				
2. Short Short Short Long				
3. Long Long Long Short				
4. Short Short Short Long				
5. Short Long Short Long				
6. Long Short Short Short				
7. Long Long Long Short				
8. Short Long Short Short				
9. Long Long Long Long				
10. Long Short Short Long				
11. Long Short Short Long				
12. Short Short Long Short				
13. Long Short Long Short				
14. Short Short Short Long				
15. Short Short Long Long				
16. Long Short Long Long				
17. Short Short Short Short				
18. Short Long Short Short				
19. Long Short Short Short				
20. Long Short Short Long				
	20	20	20	20
	%	%	%	%

Observations:

Task R: Five-Unit Repetition in Noise

Goal: The student will repeat duration patterns in noise with 90% or greater accuracy.

You will hear a sound pattern and some noise. Repeat the pattern you hear.

	Dates				
1.	Long Short Long Long Short				
2.	Short Short Long Long Long				
3.	Long Short Long Short Long				
4.	Short Short Short Short Long				
5.	Long Short Long Long Short				
6.	Short Long Short Long Long				
7.	Long Long Long Short Long				
8.	Short Short Short Long Long				
9.	Long Short Long Short Long				
10.	Short Long Short Long Long				
11.	Long Long Short Short Long				
12.	Short Long Long Long Short				
13.	Long Short Long Long Short				
14.	Long Short Short Short Long				
15.	Short Long Long Short Short				
16.	Short Long Short Short Short				
17.	Long Short Long Long Long				
18.	Long Long Short Short Long				
19.	Long Short Short Short Short				
20.	Short Short Long Long Short				
		20	20	20	20
		%	%	%	%

Observations:

Section Three: Auditory Discrimination

Auditory discrimination describes the ability to recognize acoustic differences in sounds. As we listen throughout the day, the brain constantly interprets the sounds we hear as either speech sound or non-speech sound. The brain has learned through experience that the hum of the refrigerator does not fit into the speech sound category. The temporal patterning skills the brain uses to determine that it is the refrigerator humming, instead of the microwave running, show sound discrimination and interpretation. These skills, when applied to speech sounds, can be maximized to improve perception and discrimination of the speech sounds, even when the speech sound production is distorted. These abilities are especially important with blended sounds and ongoing speech.

The sets of tasks in this section focus on training auditory discrimination skills for speech sounds. Tasks with both syllables and words are provided. Students learn skills targeting vowel differences, consonant differences, compound word contrasts, and auditory vigilance (maintaining attention for a specific target).

Note: In the compound word tasks, since the skill focus is on meaning rather than spelling, compound words selected are linguistic units consisting of at least two free forms (e.g., *sunlight, stop sign*).

Students should initially learn auditory skills in a quiet setting, free from both auditory and visual distractions. Once proficiency is mastered, the students may practice in the presence of background noise, first in steady background noise and then in variable background noise. Steady background noise is often encountered in the classroom with ventilation units, fans, and electrical equipment hum. Variable background noise includes desk or paper shuffling, pencil-sharpening, group work activities, and any situation where more than one person is talking at a time. Both of these noise conditions increase the challenge of listening and may overwhelm a student who already struggles with hearing speech.

The tasks in this section are designed with this quiet to noise hierarchy in mind. You can easily add steady background noise to the task by tuning a radio to static. Turn the noise to a level just softer than your voice/sounds. You can create variable background noise by tuning the radio to a station. As individual students differ in skills, try using a talk-radio station and then a music station. Again, turn the noise to a level just softer than your voice/sounds.

A specific goal is listed on each practice page. A performance grid is also provided on each page to track student performance. Mark a + for each correct answer and a – for each incorrect response. Monitor errors for any pattern and adjust material accordingly. A pronunciation guide is provided below for use in syllable tasks.

Pronunciation Guide		
θ (thin)	æ (cat)	ʌ (cub)
ʃ (fish)	ɛ (bet)	ʊ (book)
ŋ (wing)	ɑ (father)	e (way)
tʃ (itch)	ɪ (hid)	o (toe)
dʒ (jail)	i (me)	
ɔ (awl)	u (hoot)	

Unit One: Vowel Contrasts

Unit Two: Consonant Contrasts

Section Three: Auditory Discrimination

Unit Three: Compound Word Contrasts

Unit Four: Auditory Vigilance

Task A: Discrimination of Vowel Changes in Syllables

Goal: The student will discriminate syllables with contrasting vowels in quiet with 90% or greater accuracy.

You will hear two syllables. Tell me if the syllables are the same (S) or different (D).

	Dates				
1.	/θo/ – /θo/	(S)			
2.	/kæ/ – /kɛ/	(D)			
3.	/ɑz/ – /ɑz/	(S)			
4.	/ɪb/ – /ɪb/	(S)			
5.	/tɑ/ – /tɛ/	(D)			
6.	/ɑm/ – /om/	(D)			
7.	/pɑ/ – /pɑ/	(S)			
8.	/ʌŋ/ – /ɔŋ/	(D)			
9.	/gi/ – /gi/	(S)			
10.	/ʃʊ/ – /ʃɔ/	(D)			
11.	/lɑ/ – /lɑ/	(S)			
12.	/dæ/ – /dæ/	(S)			
13.	/mɑ/ – /mʊ/	(D)			
14.	/hʌ/ – /hʌ/	(S)			
15.	/tʃɪ/ – /tʃɔ/	(D)			
16.	/od/ – /ɪd/	(D)			
17.	/ɑt/ – /ɑt/	(S)			
18.	/oŋ/ – /oŋ/	(S)			
19.	/di/ – /di/	(S)			
20.	/mu/ – /mʊ/	(D)			
			20	20	20	20
			%	%	%	%

Observations:

Task B: Discrimination of Vowel Changes in Syllables in Noise

Goal: The student will discriminate syllables with contrasting vowels in noise with 90% or greater accuracy.

You will hear two syllables. Tell me if the syllables are the same (S) or different (D).

	Dates				
1.	/ko/ – /ki/ (D)				
2.	/dæ/ – /de/ (D)				
3.	/gɑ/ – /gɑ/ (S)				
4.	/ɪdʒ/ – /ɪdʒ/ (S)				
5.	/dɑ/ – /dɛ/ (D)				
6.	/om/ – /om/ (S)				
7.	/lɑ/ – /lɑ/ (S)				
8.	/ʌg/ – /ɔg/ (D)				
9.	/θi/ – /θi/ (S)				
10.	/ʃʊ/ – /ʃɔ/ (D)				
11.	/ʃɑ/ – /ʃɑ/ (S)				
12.	/dɪ/ – /dɪ/ (S)				
13.	/ɑt/ – /ɑt/ (S)				
14.	/hʌ/ – /hʌ/ (S)				
15.	/bɪ/ – /bɔ/ (D)				
16.	/di/ – /di/ (S)				
17.	/mɑ/ – /mʊ/ (D)				
18.	/go/ – /go/ (S)				
19.	/id/ – /ɪd/ (D)				
20.	/fu/ – /fʊ/ (D)				
		20 %	20 %	20 %	20 %

Observations:

Task C: One-Syllable Repetition

Goal: The student will repeat syllables in quiet with 90% or greater accuracy.

You will hear a syllable. Say the syllable you hear.

	Dates				
1.	/θɑ/				
2.	/næ/				
3.	/zɛ/				
4.	/ɪm/				
5.	/pɑ/				
6.	/ɑb/				
7.	/uʤ/				
8.	/ʌf/				
9.	/ri/				
10.	/ʃʊ/				
11.	/tɑ/				
12.	/kæ/				
13.	/mʊ/				
14.	/hʌ/				
15.	/bɪ/				
16.	/ɛd/				
17.	/ɑtʃ/				
18.	/bɔ/				
19.	/di/				
20.	/hʊ/				
		20	20	20	20
		%	%	%	%

Observations:

Task D: One-Syllable Repetition in Noise

Goal: The student will repeat syllables in noise with 90% or greater accuracy.

You will hear a syllable and some noise. Say the syllable you hear.

	Dates				
1.	/θɑ/				
2.	/næ/				
3.	/zo/				
4.	/ɪm/				
5.	/pɑ/				
6.	/ʤi/				
7.	/uk/				
8.	/ʌf/				
9.	/bɔ/				
10.	/kʊ/				
11.	/ɑp/				
12.	/pæ/				
13.	/mʊ/				
14.	/dʌ/				
15.	/bɪ/				
16.	/ɛd/				
17.	/ɪŋ/				
18.	/ri/				
19.	/itʃ/				
20.	/ʊt/				
		20	20	20	20
		%	%	%	%

Observations:

Task E: Discrimination of Vowel Changes in Words

(High Vowels vs. Low Vowels)

Goal: The student will discriminate words with contrasting vowels in quiet with 90% or greater accuracy.

You will hear two words. Tell me if the words are the same (S) or different (D).

	Dates				
1.	heat – hat (D)				
2.	beat – beat (S)				
3.	fat – feet (D)				
4.	tooth – tooth (S)				
5.	hop – hoop (D)				
6.	cat – cat (S)				
7.	mat – meet (D)				
8.	pop – pop (S)				
9.	droop – drop (D)				
10.	book – book (S)				
11.	dock – duke (D)				
12.	pack – peak (D)				
13.	deep – deep (S)				
14.	tan – tan (S)				
15.	bad – bead (D)				
16.	map – map (S)				
17.	fruit – fruit (S)				
18.	lock – leak (D)				
19.	weed – weed (S)				
20.	tan – teen (D)				
		20	20	20	20
		%	%	%	%

Observations:

Task F: Discrimination of Vowel Changes in Words in Noise

(High Vowels vs. Low Vowels)

Goal: The student will discriminate words with contrasting vowels in noise with 90% or greater accuracy.

You will hear two words and some noise. Tell me if the words are the same (S) or different (D).

	Dates				
1.	bad – bad	(S)			
2.	heed – had	(D)			
3.	meet – mat	(D)			
4.	scoop – scoop	(S)			
5.	hop – hoop	(D)			
6.	rat – rat	(S)			
7.	peel – pal	(D)			
8.	hot – hot	(S)			
9.	knees – knees	(S)			
10.	leaf – laugh	(D)			
11.	sleep – sleep	(S)			
12.	reach – reach	(S)			
13.	bat – beat	(D)			
14.	keys – keys	(S)			
15.	bad – bead	(D)			
16.	math – math	(S)			
17.	ham – ham	(S)			
18.	latch – leech	(D)			
19.	sop – soup	(D)			
20.	freeze – freeze	(S)			
			20	20	20	20
			%	%	%	%

Observations:

Task G: Two-Word Repetition with Changing Vowels

(High Vowels vs. Low Vowels)

Goal: The student will repeat words with contrasting vowels in quiet with 90% or greater accuracy.

You will hear two words. Say the words in the order you hear them.

Dates				
1. hot – hoot				
2. patch – peach				
3. clean – clan				
4. flat – fleet				
5. tot – toot				
6. sneak – snack				
7. batch – beach				
8. shoot – shot				
9. whack – weak				
10. rude – rod				
11. lack – leak				
12. peek – pack				
13. sod – sued				
14. man – mean				
15. cram – cream				
16. heat – hat				
17. scratch – screech				
18. hoop – hop				
19. deed – dad				
20. plaid – plead				
	20	20	20	20
	%	%	%	%

Observations:

Task H: Two-Word Repetition with Changing Vowels in Noise

(High Vowels vs. Low Vowels)

Goal: The student will repeat words with contrasting vowels in noise with 90% or greater accuracy.

You will hear two words and some noise. Say the words in the order you hear them.

Dates				
1. fleet – flat				
2. leaf – laugh				
3. drop – droop				
4. beak – back				
5. sad – seed				
6. beach – batch				
7. duke – dock				
8. pack – peek				
9. beat – bat				
10. lass – lease				
11. pat – peat				
12. laugh – leaf				
13. creak – crack				
14. rack – reek				
15. man – mean				
16. hoot – hot				
17. bad – bead				
18. shot – shoot				
19. feet – fat				
20. gnat – neat				
	20	20	20	20
	%	%	%	%

Observations:

Task I: Discrimination of Vowel Changes in Words

(Front Vowels vs. Back Vowels)

Goal: The student will discriminate words with contrasting vowels in quiet with 90% or greater accuracy.

You will hear two words. Tell me if the words are the same (S) or different (D).

	Dates				
1.	full – fill	(D)			
2.	bait – bait	(S)			
3.	low – lay	(D)			
4.	tea – tea	(S)			
5.	food – feed	(D)			
6.	clean – clean	(S)			
7.	leak – leak	(S)			
8.	doe – day	(D)			
9.	caught – caught	(S)			
10.	mitt – mitt	(S)			
11.	hoot – heat	(D)			
12.	woe – way	(D)			
13.	cream – cream	(S)			
14.	drew – drew	(S)			
15.	lick – look	(D)			
16.	beast – boost	(D)			
17.	pit – put	(D)			
18.	wheat – wheat	(S)			
19.	coat – coat	(S)			
20.	bull – bull	(S)			
			20	20	20	20
			%	%	%	%

Observations:

Task J: Discrimination of Vowel Changes in Words in Noise

(Front Vowels vs. Back Vowels)

Goal: The student will discriminate words with contrasting vowels in noise with 90% or greater accuracy.

You will hear two words and some noise. Tell me if the words are the same (S) or different (D).

		Dates				
1.	beard – beard	(S)				
2.	broad – bread	(D)				
3.	kit – kit	(S)				
4.	chest – chest	(S)				
5.	mean – moon	(D)				
6.	wait – wait	(S)				
7.	could – kid	(D)				
8.	lute – lute	(S)				
9.	stay – stow	(D)				
10.	glue – glue	(S)				
11.	wit – wit	(S)				
12.	shoe – she	(D)				
13.	boat – bait	(D)				
14.	hat – hat	(S)				
15.	nay – know	(D)				
16.	pull – pill	(D)				
17.	wig – wig	(S)				
18.	fleet – flute	(D)				
19.	big – big	(S)				
20.	twin – twin	(S)				
			20	20	20	20
			%	%	%	%

Observations:

Auditory Discrimination
Copyright © 2007 LinguiSystems, Inc.
Unit One: Vowel Contrasts
Differential Processing Training Program: Acoustic Tasks

Task K: Two-Word Repetition with Changing Vowels

(Front Vowels vs. Back Vowels)

Goal: The student will repeat words with contrasting vowels in quiet with 90% or greater accuracy.

You will hear two words. Say the words in the order you hear them.

	Dates				
1.	lean – loon				
2.	fled – flawed				
3.	brick – brook				
4.	bone – bean				
5.	reed – rude				
6.	slay – slow				
7.	tool – teal				
8.	bin – bone				
9.	they – though				
10.	cook – kick				
11.	laud – led				
12.	she – shoe				
13.	brewed – bread				
14.	geese – goose				
15.	flew – flea				
16.	bait – boat				
17.	foot – fit				
18.	hoe – hay				
19.	beet – boot				
20.	steal – stool				
		20	20	20	20
		%	%	%	%

Observations:

Task L: Two-Word Repetition with Changing Vowels in Noise (Front Vowels vs. Back Vowels)

Goal: The student will repeat words with contrasting vowels in noise with 90% or greater accuracy.

You will hear two words and some noise. Say the words in the order you hear them.

Dates				
1. flute – fleet				
2. moon – mean				
3. read – rude				
4. teal – tool				
5. boot – beet				
6. breed – brewed				
7. stool – steel				
8. scene – soon				
9. led – laud				
10. wool – will				
11. foot – fit				
12. bait – boat				
13. stay – stow				
14. bruise – breeze				
15. she – shoe				
16. boost – beast				
17. team – tomb				
18. though – they				
19. fled – flawed				
20. look – lick				
	20 %	20 %	20 %	20 %

Observations:

Task A: Discrimination of Initial Consonant Changes in Words (High Frequency vs. Low Frequency Consonants)

Goal: The student will discriminate words with contrasting consonants in quiet with 90% or greater accuracy.

You will hear two words. Tell me if the words are the same (S) or different (D).

		Dates				
1.	cat – cat	(S)				
2.	foam – dome	(D)				
3.	like – like	(S)				
4.	seat – beet	(D)				
5.	vase – face	(D)				
6.	maid – maid	(S)				
7.	bake – fake	(D)				
8.	dirt – dirt	(S)				
9.	bin – thin	(D)				
10.	seed – need	(D)				
11.	loot – loot	(S)				
12.	band – band	(S)				
13.	five – dive	(D)				
14.	men – men	(S)				
15.	loop – soup	(D)				
16.	knit – knit	(S)				
17.	sour – sour	(S)				
18.	coal – bowl	(D)				
19.	band – sand	(D)				
20.	lip – lip	(S)				
			20	20	20	20
			%	%	%	%

Observations:

Task B: Discrimination of Initial Consonant Changes in Words in Noise (High Frequency vs. Low Frequency Consonants)

Goal: The student will discriminate words with contrasting consonants in noise with 90% or greater accuracy.

You will hear two words and some noise. Tell me if the words are the same (S) or different (D).

	Dates				
1.	catch – match (D)				
2.	beep – beep (S)				
3.	keys – keys (S)				
4.	thighs – buys (D)				
5.	vine – sign (D)				
6.	bug – bug (S)				
7.	dial – file (D)				
8.	beam – theme (D)				
9.	soft – soft (S)				
10.	belt – felt (D)				
11.	cord – cord (S)				
12.	thing – ding (D)				
13.	four – four (S)				
14.	lug – lug (S)				
15.	mail – sail (D)				
16.	belt – belt (S)				
17.	light – fight (D)				
18.	this – miss (D)				
19.	bone – bone (S)				
20.	seek – beak (D)				
		20	20	20	20
		%	%	%	%

Observations:

Copyright © 2007 LinguiSystems, Inc.

Unit Two: Consonant Contrasts
Differential Processing Training Program: Acoustic Tasks

Task C: Two-Word Repetition with Changing Initial Consonants (High Frequency vs. Low Frequency Consonants)

Goal: The student will repeat words with contrasting consonants in quiet with 90% or greater accuracy.

You will hear two words. Say the words in the order you hear them.

Dates				
1. that – bat				
2. name – same				
3. late – fate				
4. mend – send				
5. those – doze				
6. kilt – built				
7. neat – feet				
8. soup – loop				
9. bead – feed				
10. lace – case				
11. zinc – think				
12. this – miss				
13. came – lame				
14. noon – soon				
15. cord – bored				
16. size – lies				
17. felt – dealt				
18. sat – vat				
19. cob – knob				
20. keel – meal				
	20	20	20	20
	%	%	%	%

Observations:

Task D: Two-Word Repetition with Changing Initial Consonants in Noise (High Frequency vs. Low Frequency Consonants)

Goal: The student will repeat words with contrasting consonants in noise with 90% or greater accuracy.

You will hear two words and some noise. Say the words in the order you hear them.

Dates				
1. felt – belt				
2. sag – bag				
3. mat – sat				
4. sews – doze				
5. bus – fuss				
6. foal – knoll				
7. beam – seam				
8. set – let				
9. dot – cot				
10. cop – mop				
11. fin – bin				
12. mob – cob				
13. lock – sock				
14. sad – dad				
15. sand – band				
16. deal – feel				
17. fox – box				
18. bull – full				
19. dog – fog				
20. lick – sick				
	20	20	20	20
	%	%	%	%

Observations:

Task E: Discrimination of Initial Consonant Cluster Changes in Words (High Frequency vs. Low Frequency Consonants)

Goal: The student will discriminate words with contrasting consonants in quiet with 90% or greater accuracy.

You will hear two words. Tell me if the words are the same (S) or different (D).

	Dates					
1.	flap – flap	(S)				
2.	bring – bring	(S)				
3.	fried – dried	(D)				
4.	draft – craft	(D)				
5.	broom – broom	(S)				
6.	brown – frown	(D)				
7.	drew – drew	(S)				
8.	slack – black	(D)				
9.	frayed – braid	(D)				
10.	dress – dress	(S)				
11.	scarf – scarf	(S)				
12.	threw – drew	(D)				
13.	bloom – bloom	(S)				
14.	crumb – drum	(D)				
15.	stick – stick	(S)				
16.	draw – draw	(S)				
17.	blush – flush	(D)				
18.	crawl – drawl	(D)				
19.	dream – dream	(S)				
20.	breeze – freeze	(D)				
			20	20	20	20
			%	%	%	%

Observations:

Task F: Discrimination of Initial Consonant Cluster Changes in Words in Noise (High Frequency vs. Low Frequency Consonants)

Goal: The student will discriminate words with contrasting consonants in noise with 90% or greater accuracy.

You will hear two words and some noise. Tell me if the words are the same (S) or different (D).

	Dates				
1.	drain – drain (S)				
2.	crack – black (D)				
3.	bride – bride (S)				
4.	flame – blame (D)				
5.	fry – dry (D)				
6.	draft – draft (S)				
7.	slush – slush (S)				
8.	phrase – braise (D)				
9.	breeze – breeze (S)				
10.	brown – clown (D)				
11.	crew – drew (D)				
12.	drill – thrill (D)				
13.	fleet – fleet (S)				
14.	drip – drip (S)				
15.	thread – bread (D)				
16.	stick – stick (S)				
17.	fruit – fruit (S)				
18.	crown – brown (D)				
19.	bled – sled (D)				
20.	blast – blast (S)				
		20	20	20	20
		%	%	%	%

Observations:

Task G: Two-Word Repetition with Changing Initial Consonant Clusters (Change in Second Phoneme of the Consonant Cluster)

Goal: The student will repeat words with contrasting consonants in quiet with 90% or greater accuracy.

You will hear two words. Say the words in the order you hear them.

Dates				
1. grow – glow				
2. crack – clack				
3. breed – bleed				
4. crime – climb				
5. snow – slow				
6. bloom – broom				
7. clam – cram				
8. proud – plowed				
9. snare – stare				
10. flies – fries				
11. frame – flame				
12. scoop – stoop				
13. play – pray				
14. spot – slot				
15. blues – bruise				
16. stool – spool				
17. scope – slope				
18. prank – plank				
19. blush – brush				
20. clue – crew				
	20	20	20	20
	%	%	%	%

Observations:

Task H: Two-Word Repetition with Changing Initial Consonant Clusters in Noise (Change in Second Phoneme of the Consonant Cluster)

Goal: The student will repeat words with contrasting consonants in noise with 90% or greater accuracy.

You will hear two words and some noise. Say the words in the order you hear them.

Dates				
1. blade – braid				
2. glade – grade				
3. slack – snack				
4. flesh – fresh				
5. smell – spell				
6. bleach – breach				
7. crash – clash				
8. slow – snow				
9. grew – glue				
10. flea – free				
11. sleek – sneak				
12. graze – glaze				
13. spore – snore				
14. clown – crown				
15. breed – bleed				
16. sneak – speak				
17. plank – prank				
18. crime – climb				
19. brand – bland				
20. smoke – spoke				
	20	20	20	20
	%	%	%	%

Observations:

Task I: Two-Word Repetition with Changing Initial Consonant Clusters (High Frequency vs. Low Frequency Consonants)

Goal: The student will repeat words with contrasting consonants in quiet with 90% or greater accuracy.

You will hear two words. Say the words in the order you hear them.

Dates				
1. slow – blow				
2. threw – drew				
3. block – flock				
4. cream – dream				
5. freeze – breeze				
6. bled – sled				
7. throne – drone				
8. blare – flare				
9. from – crumb				
10. bread – thread				
11. slack – black				
12. try – dry				
13. drop – crop				
14. blood – flood				
15. crane – drain				
16. bright – fright				
17. frill – drill				
18. blot – slot				
19. draft – craft				
20. flush – blush				
	20	20	20	20
	%	%	%	%

Observations:

Task J: Two-Word Repetition with Changing Initial Consonant Clusters in Noise (High Frequency vs. Low Frequency Consonants)

Goal: The student will repeat words with contrasting consonants in noise with 90% or greater accuracy.

You will hear two words and some noise. Say the words in the order you hear them.

Dates				
1. blown – flown				
2. spill – drill				
3. clock – block				
4. three – brie				
5. dry – fry				
6. brain – crane				
7. crop – drop				
8. dream – cream				
9. drill – thrill				
10. cruise – bruise				
11. flame – blame				
12. drown – crown				
13. black – slack				
14. sleet – bleat				
15. broad – fraud				
16. slow – blow				
17. thread – bread				
18. brewed – crude				
19. drain – crane				
20. fleet – bleat				
	20 / %	20 / %	20 / %	20 / %

Observations:

Task K: Discrimination of Initial Consonant Cluster Reduction

Goal: The student will discriminate words with contrasting consonants in quiet with 90% or greater accuracy.

You will hear two words. Tell me if the words are the same (S) or different (D).

	Dates				
1.	brick – brick	(S)			
2.	skip – sip	(D)			
3.	brook – book	(D)			
4.	fresh – fresh	(S)			
5.	snail – sail	(D)			
6.	crop – crop	(S)			
7.	glass – gas	(D)			
8.	flight – fight	(D)			
9.	grape – grape	(S)			
10.	dress – dress	(S)			
11.	please – peas	(D)			
12.	prop – prop	(S)			
13.	sting – sting	(S)			
14.	scum – scum	(S)			
15.	trail – tail	(D)			
16.	snip – snip	(S)			
17.	bread – bed	(D)			
18.	sport – sort	(D)			
19.	clamp – camp	(D)			
20.	twin – twin	(S)			
			20	20	20	20
			%	%	%	%

Observations:

Task L: Discrimination of Initial Consonant Cluster Reduction in Noise

Goal: The student will discriminate words with contrasting consonants in noise with 90% or greater accuracy.

You will hear two words in noise. Tell me if the words are the same (S) or different (D).

	Dates				
1.	treat – treat	(S)			
2.	snack – sack	(D)			
3.	stew – stew	(S)			
4.	freeze – fees	(D)			
5.	stink – sink	(D)			
6.	truck – truck	(S)			
7.	trip – tip	(D)			
8.	snore – snore	(S)			
9.	track – tack	(D)			
10.	crave – crave	(S)			
11.	frog – fog	(D)			
12.	stock – sock	(D)			
13.	price – price	(S)			
14.	pry – pie	(D)			
15.	free – free	(S)			
16.	plain – pain	(D)			
17.	brat – brat	(S)			
18.	flap – flap	(S)			
19.	brace – base	(D)			
20.	drive – dive	(D)			
			20	20	20	20
			%	%	%	%

Observations:

Task M: Two-Word Repetition with Initial Cluster Reduction

Goal: The student will repeat words with contrasting consonants in quiet with 90% or greater accuracy.

You will hear two words. Say the words in the order you hear them.

Dates				
1. stone – sewn				
2. blows – bows				
3. steal – seal				
4. crash – cash				
5. speed – seed				
6. place – pace				
7. breeze – bees				
8. claim – came				
9. true – two				
10. bleed – bead				
11. cling – king				
12. grill – gill				
13. frog – fog				
14. stray – stay				
15. grass – gas				
16. sprite – spite				
17. scream – scheme				
18. prose – pose				
19. grape – gape				
20. stream – steam				
	20	20	20	20
	%	%	%	%

Observations:

Task N: Two-Word Repetition with Initial Cluster Reduction in Noise

Goal: The student will repeat words with contrasting consonants in noise with 90% or greater accuracy.

You will hear two words and some noise. Say the words in the order you hear them.

Dates				
1. grow – go				
2. blank – bank				
3. flea – fee				
4. brass – bass				
5. scoop – soup				
6. trip – tip				
7. fled – fed				
8. track – tack				
9. clap – cap				
10. truck – tuck				
11. scale – sail				
12. drew – dew				
13. grate – gate				
14. clash – cash				
15. bleach – beach				
16. tree – tea				
17. grease – geese				
18. skunk – sunk				
19. freight – fate				
20. slick – sick				
	20	20	20	20
	%	%	%	%

Observations:

Task O: Discrimination of Final Consonant Changes in Words (High Frequency vs. Low Frequency Consonants)

Goal: The student will discriminate words with contrasting consonants in quiet with 90% or greater accuracy.

You will hear two words. Tell me if the words are the same (S) or different (D).

	Dates				
1.	cub – cub	(S)				
2.	ham – half	(D)				
3.	peel – peak	(D)				
4.	tack – tack	(S)				
5.	wine – wine	(S)				
6.	booth – boom	(D)				
7.	real – reef	(D)				
8.	sing – sing	(S)				
9.	toes – toes	(S)				
10.	safe – sale	(D)				
11.	book – book	(S)				
12.	push – push	(S)				
13.	wing – with	(D)				
14.	raid – rake	(D)				
15.	cap – cap	(S)				
16.	peel – peel	(S)				
17.	fade - face	(D)				
18.	teeth – teen	(D)				
19.	cane – cane	(S)				
20.	week – weed	(D)				
			20	20	20	20
			%	%	%	%

Observations:

Task P: Discrimination of Final Consonant Changes in Words in Noise (High Frequency vs. Low Frequency Consonants)

Goal: The student will discriminate words with contrasting consonants in noise with 90% or greater accuracy.

You will hear two words and some noise. Tell me if the words are the same (S) or different (D).

Dates				
1. cube – cube (S)				
2. chief – chief (S)				
3. tough – tub (D)				
4. dove – dove (S)				
5. pun – puff (D)				
6. click – click (S)				
7. stud – stuck (D)				
8. both – bone (D)				
9. cave – cave (S)				
10. plaque – plaid (D)				
11. make – made (D)				
12. save – save (S)				
13. seek – seed (D)				
14. rain – rain (S)				
15. slam – slack (D)				
16. lid – lid (S)				
17. wrong – wrong (S)				
18. teen – teen (S)				
19. bun – bus (D)				
20. niece – need (D)				
	20	20	20	20
	%	%	%	%

Observations:

Task Q: Two-Word Repetition with Changing Final Consonants

(High Frequency vs. Low Frequency Consonants)

Goal: The student will repeat words with contrasting consonants in quiet with 90% or greater accuracy.

You will hear two words. Say the words in the order you hear them.

Dates				
1. whiff – wing				
2. sale – safe				
3. bang – back				
4. calf – cab				
5. weed – weak				
6. case – came				
7. wreath – reed				
8. lead – leaf				
9. teeth – tease				
10. chick – chin				
11. broth – broad				
12. hum – huff				
13. hound – house				
14. grab – graph				
15. theme – thief				
16. mice – mile				
17. tomb – tooth				
18. bead – beef				
19. lung – luck				
20. froth – fraud				
	20	20	20	20
	%	%	%	%

Observations:

Task R: Two-Word Repetition with Changing Final Consonants in Noise (High Frequency vs. Low Frequency Consonants)

Goal: The student will repeat words with contrasting consonants in noise with 90% or greater accuracy.

You will hear two words and some noise. Say the words in the order you hear them.

Dates				
1. class – clam				
2. tough – tub				
3. wife – wide				
4. cook – could				
5. tab – tack				
6. house – howl				
7. wheel – week				
8. beak – bead				
9. lock – lob				
10. man – math				
11. peas – piece				
12. duck – dull				
13. rake – rain				
14. sack – sang				
15. leaf – leave				
16. cake – came				
17. poke – pole				
18. rule – roof				
19. lung – luck				
20. bath – bad				
	20	20	20	20
	%	%	%	%

Observations:

Task S: Discrimination of Final Consonant Cluster Changes in Words

Goal: The student will discriminate words with contrasting consonants in quiet with 90% or greater accuracy.

You will hear two words. Tell me if the words are the same (S) or different (D).

		Dates				
1.	tent – tent	(S)				
2.	mind – mild	(D)				
3.	belt – bent	(D)				
4.	silk – silk	(S)				
5.	craft – craft	(S)				
6.	lift – lint	(D)				
7.	boils – boils	(S)				
8.	taps – tacks	(D)				
9.	bold – bond	(D)				
10.	hunt – hunt	(S)				
11.	salt – soft	(D)				
12.	jump – jump	(S)				
13.	stuffs – stubs	(D)				
14.	meant – melt	(D)				
15.	fast – fact	(D)				
16.	grills – grills	(S)				
17.	clicks – cliffs	(D)				
18.	twist – twist	(S)				
19.	sets – sets	(S)				
20.	loft – lost	(D)				
			20	20	20	20
			%	%	%	%

Observations:

Task T: Discrimination of Final Consonant Cluster Changes in Words in Noise

Goal: The student will discriminate words with contrasting consonants in noise with 90% or greater accuracy.

You will hear two words and some noise. Tell me if the words are the same (S) or different (D).

	Dates				
1.	prompt – prompt (S)				
2.	steaks – states (D)				
3.	crisp – crisp (S)				
4.	mint – mist (D)				
5.	bills – bids (D)				
6.	skunk – skunk (S)				
7.	front – front (S)				
8.	tint – tilt (D)				
9.	wild – wind (D)				
10.	pump – pump (S)				
11.	tricks – trips (D)				
12.	barked – barked (S)				
13.	shift – shift (S)				
14.	parts – pants (D)				
15.	smash – smash (S)				
16.	toast – toast (S)				
17.	backs – bats (D)				
18.	disk – disk (S)				
19.	necks – nests (D)				
20.	spend – spend (S)				
		20	20	20	20
		%	%	%	%

Observations:

Task U: Two-Word Repetition with Changing Final Consonant Clusters

Goal: The student will repeat words with contrasting consonants in quiet with 90% or greater accuracy.

You will hear two words. Say the words in the order you hear them.

Dates				
1. stable – staple				
2. rumble – rumple				
3. mask – mark				
4. docks – dots				
5. runs – rubs				
6. pods – pots				
7. wraps – rats				
8. spooks – spoofs				
9. tricks – trims				
10. cheats – cheeps				
11. beeps – beefs				
12. mast – mask				
13. stuffs – stubs				
14. rooms – roofs				
15. caps – cats				
16. ant – act				
17. seeps – seats				
18. fact – fast				
19. bend – bent				
20. nests – necks				
	20	20	20	20
	%	%	%	%

Observations:

Task V: Two-Word Repetition with Changing Final Consonant Clusters in Noise

Goal: The student will repeat words with contrasting consonants in noise with 90% or greater accuracy.

You will hear two words and some noise. Say the words in the order you hear them.

Dates				
1. clamp – clasp				
2. rocks – rots				
3. cask – cast				
4. maps – mats				
5. bills – bids				
6. spins – spills				
7. forks – forts				
8. parts – pants				
9. tricks – trims				
10. dusk – dust				
11. cliffs – clips				
12. naps – gnats				
13. creams – creaks				
14. mend – meant				
15. bumps – buffs				
16. wrist – risk				
17. fact – fast				
18. sips – sits				
19. cranes – crates				
20. cuts – cups				
	20	20	20	20
	%	%	%	%

Observations:

Task A: Discrimination of Compound Words

Goal: The student will discriminate compound words in quiet with 90% or greater accuracy.

You will hear two words. Tell me if the words are the same (S) or different (D).

	Dates					
1.	barefoot – barefoot	(S)				
2.	stop sign – stoplight	(D)				
3.	footstep – footprint	(D)				
4.	goldfish – goldfish	(S)				
5.	bathrobe – bathtub	(D)				
6.	time clock – time clock	(S)				
7.	bookstore – bookworm	(D)				
8.	lifeguard – lifeguard	(S)				
9.	sunlight – sunrise	(D)				
10.	airport – airplane	(D)				
11.	bookmark – bookmark	(S)				
12.	watermelon – watercolor	(D)				
13.	lunchroom – lunchroom	(S)				
14.	overgrow – overflow	(D)				
15.	homesick – homeroom	(D)				
16.	popcorn – popcorn	(S)				
17.	flashlight – flashlight	(S)				
18.	haircut – haircut	(S)				
19.	backpack – backbone	(D)				
20.	football – football	(S)				
			20	20	20	20
			%	%	%	%

Observations:

Task B: Discrimination of Compound Words in Noise

Goal: The student will discriminate compound words in noise with 90% or greater accuracy.

You will hear two words and some noise. Tell me if the words are the same (S) or different (D).

	Dates					
1.	story time – storybook	(D)				
2.	shoelace – shoelace	(S)				
3.	underground – underwater	(D)				
4.	headlight – headphones	(D)				
5.	sailboat – sailboat	(S)				
6.	railroad – railroad	(S)				
7.	toothpaste – toothbrush	(D)				
8.	headache – headache	(S)				
9.	eggshell – eggplant	(D)				
10.	fire truck – fire hose	(D)				
11.	barefoot – barefoot	(S)				
12.	reindeer – reindeer	(S)				
13.	doorstep – doorbell	(D)				
14.	fireworks – firewood	(D)				
15.	farmland – farmland	(S)				
16.	oversleep – oversleep	(S)				
17.	snowplow – snowflake	(D)				
18.	campfire – campfire	(S)				
19.	horseshoe – horseshoe	(S)				
20.	race boat – racecar	(D)				
			20	20	20	20
			%	%	%	%

Observations:

Task C: Two-Word Repetition with Compound Words

Goal: The student will repeat compound words in quiet with 90% or greater accuracy.

You will hear two words. Say the words in the order you hear them.

	Dates				
1.	spaceship – spacecraft				
2.	backpack – backstroke				
3.	handshake – handball				
4.	footprint – footstep				
5.	waterfall – waterbed				
6.	light bulb – lighthouse				
7.	fireplace – firewood				
8.	headphone – headlight				
9.	toothbrush – toothpaste				
10.	fire hose – fire truck				
11.	fishhook – fishpond				
12.	school bus – school bell				
13.	meatball – meatloaf				
14.	earring – earplug				
15.	downhill – downstream				
16.	airport – airmail				
17.	billboard – billfold				
18.	spaceman – spacewalk				
19.	fireworks – firecracker				
20.	snowboard – snowplow				
		20	20	20	20
		%	%	%	%

Observations:

Task D: Two-Word Repetition with Compound Words in Noise

Goal: The student will repeat compound words in noise with 90% or greater accuracy.

You will hear two words and some noise. Say the words in the order you hear them.

	Dates				
1.	grapefruit – grapevine				
2.	scoreboard – scorekeeper				
3.	lawnmower – lawn chair				
4.	rainbow – raindrop				
5.	motorcycle – motorbike				
6.	ballroom – ballpark				
7.	waterproof – watermark				
8.	underhand – underfoot				
9.	flypaper – flyswatter				
10.	airbrush – airtight				
11.	fingernail – fingerprint				
12.	pinecone – pineapple				
13.	skyscraper – skyline				
14.	thumbprint – thumbtack				
15.	sunshine – sunburn				
16.	nightgown – nightlight				
17.	hairspray – hairbrush				
18.	cowboy – cowgirl				
19.	dishwasher – dishpan				
20.	bathtub – bathroom				
		20	20	20	20
		%	%	%	%

Observations:

Auditory Discrimination
Copyright © 2007 LinguiSystems, Inc.

Unit Three: Compound Word Contrasts
Differential Processing Training Program: Acoustic Tasks

Task E: Chaining Repetition with Compound Words

Goal: The student will repeat compound words in quiet with 90% or greater accuracy.

You will hear some words. Say the words in the order you hear them.

	Dates				
1.	sandpaper – paperweight				
2.	headlight – light bulb				
3.	crabmeat – meatloaf				
4.	pitchfork – forklift				
5.	snowsuit – suitcase				
6.	sunflower – flowerpot				
7.	airmail – mail carrier				
8.	kettledrum – drumstick				
9.	lumberjack – jackhammer				
10.	jellyfish – fishbowl				
11.	bobcat – cattail – tailwind				
12.	scoreboard – boardwalk – walkway				
13.	rainwater – water gun – gun shy				
14.	stickpin – pinwheel – wheelbarrow				
15.	shortstop – stoplight – lighthouse				
16.	backdoor – doorstep – stepstool				
17.	popcorn – cornfield – fieldwork				
18.	sawdust – dustpan – pancake				
19.	mailbox – boxcar – carport				
20.	blackbird – birdhouse – houseboat				
		20	20	20	20
		%	%	%	%

Observations:

Task F: Chaining Repetition with Compound Words in Noise

Goal: The student will repeat compound words in noise with 90% or greater accuracy.

You will hear some words and some noise. Say the words in the order you hear them.

	Dates				
1.	volleyball – ballgame				
2.	airbrush – brushstroke				
3.	grapefruit – fruitcake				
4.	daydream – dream weaver				
5.	yearbook – bookmark				
6.	underarm – armhole				
7.	rattlesnake – snakeskin				
8.	swordfish – fishpond				
9.	oatmeal – mealworm				
10.	pinwheel – wheelbarrow				
11.	sand trap – trapdoor – doorbell				
12.	backhand – handgun – gunshot				
13.	driveway – wayside – sideboard				
14.	eardrum – drumstick – stick-up				
15.	starlight – lighthouse – housecoat				
16.	sawhorse – horseshoe – shoehorn				
17.	pineapple – applesauce – saucepan				
18.	sandpaper – paperback – backstop				
19.	barefoot – footstep – stepstool				
20.	redhead – headboard – boardwalk				
		20	20	20	20
		%	%	%	%

Observations:

Task A: Discrimination of Syllables in One-Contrast Strings

Goal: The student will identify target syllables in syllable strings in quiet with 90% or greater accuracy.

You will hear some syllables. Every time you hear the syllable _____, raise your hand. (You can say the syllables with either a long or short vowel, but be consistent through the rest of the sound string.)

			Dates				
1.	(ga)	da – *ga* – da – *ga* – da – *ga* – da – *ga* – da – *ga*					
2.	(pa)	da – da – *pa* – da – da – *pa* – da – da – *pa* – da					
3.	(ta)	da – da – da – *ta* – da – da – da – *ta* – da – da					
4.	(wa)	da – da – da – da – *wa* – da – *wa* – da – da – da					
5.	(ba)	da – *ba* – da – da – da – da – da – da – *ba* – da					
6.	(ma)	da – da – da – *ma* – da – *ma* – da – da – da – *ma*					
7.	(la)	da – da – *la* – *la* – da – *la* – da – da – *la* – da					
8.	(ka)	*ka* – da – da – da – da – *ka* – da – da – da – da					
9.	(fa)	da – da – da – da – *fa* – da – da – *fa* – da – da					
10.	(ra)	da – *ra* – da – da – da – da – *ra* – da – da – *ra*					
11.	(te)	de – de – de – *te* – de – de – de – de – *te* – de					
12.	(be)	de – *be* – de – de – de – de – *be* – de – de – *be*					
13.	(ke)	de – de – de – de – *ke* – de – de – de – de – *ke*					
14.	(fe)	*fe* – de – de – de – de – de – de – *fe* – de – de					
15.	(se)	de – de – *se* – de – de – de – de – de – *se* – *se*					
16.	(we)	de – de – de – de – de – *we* – de – de – de – de					
17.	(le)	de – *le* – de – de – *le* – de – de – de – de – de					
18.	(me)	de – de – de – *me* – de – de – de – de – de – de					
19.	(ze)	de – de – *ze* – de – de – de – de – de – de – *ze*					
20.	(re)	de – de – de – de – de – de – *re* – de – de – de					
				20	20	20	20
				%	%	%	%

Observations:

Task B: Discrimination of Syllables in Multi-Contrast Strings

Goal: The student will identify target syllables in syllable strings in quiet with 90% or greater accuracy.

You will hear some syllables. Every time you hear the syllable _____, raise your hand. (You can say the syllables with either a long or short vowel, but be consistent through the rest of the sound string.)

			Dates				
1.	(ta)	da – ba – da – *ta* – ba – da – *ta* – ba – ba – *ta*					
2.	(be)	we – we – *be* – me – we – me – *be* – me – *be* – we					
3.	(ha)	ma – da – *ha* – da – da – *ha* – ma – da – ma – *ha*					
4.	(pe)	he – le – le – he – *pe* – le – *pe* – he – he – *pe*					
5.	(so)	lo – mo – ro – *so* – mo – ro – mo – lo – *so* – mo					
6.	(la)	ka – pa – *la* – ga – ka – *la* – pa – ka – *la* – ga					
7.	(re)	se – *re* – be – *re* – me – se – be – me – *re* – se					
8.	(ti)	mi – di – li – si – *ti* – wi – di – si – mi – *ti*					
9.	(da)	ga – *da* – ta – ma – fa – *da* – ma – la – ma – *da*					
10.	(he)	we – me – *he* – te – pe – me – we – pe – *he* – be					
11.	(ma)	ta – da – ka – *ma* – da – ra – da – *ma* – ra – pa					
12.	(se)	ve – *se* – me – ne – te – ve – *se* – ne – te – ve					
13.	(ka)	ha – na – la – ha – *ka* – la – ga – na – ta – ga					
14.	(hu)	tu – du – lu – *hu* – ru – *hu* – du – pu – lu – *hu*					
15.	(ba)	ra – wa – *ba* – la – ha – pa – ta – ma – *ba* – wa					
16.	(me)	ge – ke – le – *me* – pe – te – re – de – se – *me*					
17.	(bo)	lo – go – vo – lo – po – *bo* – ho – so – lo – *bo*					
18.	(ke)	ye – le – pe – he – le – ye – ve – *ke* – me – de					
19.	(zi)	bi – ri – ti – mi – *zi* – li – pi – ri – fi – mi					
20.	(hi)	pi – ti – mi – ri – fi – bi – *hi* – mi – pi – di					
			/20 %	/20 %	/20 %	/20 %	

Observations:

Copyright © 2007 LinguiSystems, Inc.
Unit Four: Auditory Vigilance
Differential Processing Training Program: Acoustic Tasks

Task C: Discrimination of Syllables in One-Contrast Strings in Noise

Goal: The student will identify target syllables in syllable strings in noise with 90% or greater accuracy.

You will hear some syllables and some noise. Every time you hear the syllable _____, raise your hand. (You can say the syllables with either a long or short vowel, but be consistent through the rest of the sound string.)

			Dates				
1.	(pa)	da – *pa* – da – *pa* – da – *pa* – da – *pa* – da – *pa*					
2.	(ga)	da – *ga* – da – da – da – da – *ga* – da – da – *ga*					
3.	(ta)	da – da – *ta* – da – da – *ta* – da – da – da – da					
4.	(wa)	da – *wa* – da – da – da – da – da – *wa* – da – da					
5.	(ba)	da – da – da – da – *ba* – da – da – *ba* – da – da					
6.	(ma)	*ma* – da – da – da – da – *ma* – da – da – *ma* – da					
7.	(la)	da – da – *la* – *la* – da – *la* – da – da – *la* – da					
8.	(ka)	da – *ka* – da – da – da – *ka* – da – da – da – da					
9.	(fa)	da – da – da – *fa* – da – da – da – *fa* – da – da					
10.	(ra)	da – *ra* – da – da – da – da – *ra* – da – da – *ra*					
11.	(te)	de – de – de – *te* – de – de – de – de – *te* – de					
12.	(be)	*be* – de – de – de – de – *be* – de – de – de – *be*					
13.	(ke)	de – de – de – de – *ke* – de – de – de – de – *ke*					
14.	(fe)	de – de – de – *fe* – de – de – de – *fe* – de – de					
15.	(se)	de – de – *se* – de – de – de – de – de – *se* – *se*					
16.	(we)	de – de – de – de – de – *we* – de – de – de – de					
17.	(le)	de – de – de – de – *le* – de – *le* – de – de – de					
18.	(me)	de – de – de – *me* – de – de – de – de – de – de					
19.	(ze)	de – de – *ze* – de – de – de – de – de – de – *ze*					
20.	(re)	de – de – de – de – de – de – de – de – *re* – de					
			20	20	20	20
			%	%	%	%

Observations:

Task D: Discrimination of Syllables in Multi-Contrast Strings in Noise

Goal: The student will identify target syllables in syllable strings in noise with 90% or greater accuracy.

You will hear some syllables and some noise. Every time you hear the syllable _____, raise your hand. (You can say the syllables with either a long or short vowel, but be consistent through the rest of the sound string.)

			Dates				
1.	(la)	ka – pa – *la* – ga – ka – *la* – pa – ka – *la* – ga					
2.	(ha)	ma – da – *ha* – da – da – *ha* – ma – da – ma – *ha*					
3.	(be)	we – we – *be* – me – we – me – *be* – me – *be* – we					
4.	(re)	se – *re* – be – *re* – me – se – be – me – *re* – se					
5.	(so)	lo – mo – ro – *so* – mo – ro – mo – lo – *so* – mo					
6.	(ta)	da – ba – da – *ta* – ba – da – *ta* – ba – ba – *ta*					
7.	(se)	ve – *se* – me – ne – te – ve – *se* – ne – te – ve					
8.	(ti)	mi – di – li – si – *ti* – wi – di – si – mi – *ti*					
9.	(ma)	ta – da – ka – *ma* – da – ra – da – *ma* – ra – pa					
10.	(he)	we – me – *he* – te – pe – me – we – pe – *he* – be					
11.	(da)	ga – *da* – ta – ma – fa – *da* – ma – la – ma – *da*					
12.	(we)	he – le – le – he – *we* – le – be – he – *we* – be					
13.	(ka)	ha – na – la – ha – *ka* – la – ga – na – ta – ga					
14.	(hu)	tu – du – lu – *hu* – ru – *hu* – du – pu – lu – *hu*					
15.	(ba)	ra – wa – *ba* – la – ha – pa – ta – ma – *ba* – wa					
16.	(ke)	ye – le – pe – he – le – ye – ve – *ke* – me – de					
17.	(bo)	lo – go – vo – lo – po – *bo* – ho – so – lo – *bo*					
18.	(me)	ge – ke – *me* – le – pe – te – re – de – se – *me*					
19.	(zi)	bi – ri – ti – mi – *zi* – li – pi – ri – fi – mi					
20.	(hi)	pi – ti – mi – ri – fi – bi – *hi* – mi – pi – di					
			20	20	20	20	
			%	%	%	%	

Observations:

Task E: Discrimination of Words in Multi-Contrast Strings

Goal: The student will identify target words in word strings in quiet with 90% or greater accuracy.

You will hear some words. Every time you hear the word _____, raise your hand.

			Dates				
1.	(lip)	sip – rip – dip – *lip* – trip – sip – *lip* – dip – tip – *lip*					
2.	(cat)	rat – bat – at – fat – *cat* – bat – pat – sat – *cat* – rat					
3.	(mop)	hop – top – *mop* – pop – top – hop – *mop* – top – *mop* – hop					
4.	(bag)	tag – wag – rag – gag – tag – *bag* – gag – lag – nag – *bag*					
5.	(toy)	joy – soy – *toy* – coy – soy – coy – *toy* – joy – coy – *toy*					
6.	(win)	fin – chin – bin – grin – pin – *win* – sin – tin – grin – bin					
7.	(pit)	sit – it – knit – *pit* – fit – bit – sit – *pit* – it – hit					
8.	(got)	hot – *got* – pot – rot – *got* – dot – jot – tot – hot – not					
9.	(sell)	tell – bell – fell – gel – yell – bell – *sell* – fell – tell – *sell*					
10.	(tack)	jack – sack – *tack* – lack – back – sack – jack – lack – *tack* – pack					
11.	(hill)	fill – *hill* – mill – dill – pill – sill – fill – dill – will – *hill*					
12.	(saw)	law – jaw – raw – law – claw – jaw – *saw* – thaw – *saw* – law					
13.	(tick)	lick – pick – wick – kick – *tick* – nick – pick – *tick* – kick – lick					
14.	(hole)	roll – dole – toll – *hole* – mole – bowl – roll – coal – pole – *hole*					
15.	(bug)	rug – *bug* – lug – jug – dug – lug – rug – mug – *bug* – hug					
16.	(pan)	man – tan – can – fan – tan – *pan* – can – man – ban – fan					
17.	(nap)	lap – tap – zap – *nap* – map – sap – cap – *nap* – zap – tap					
18.	(job)	cob – *job* – rob – cob – blob – rob – knob – mob – sob – *job*					
19.	(fun)	bun – nun – sun – run – done – one – *fun* – ton – son – gun					
20.	(hum)	yum – bum – some – *hum* – gum – yum – from – bum – *hum* – plum					
			/20	/20	/20	/20	
			%	%	%	%	

Observations:

Task F: Discrimination of Words in Multi-Contrast Strings in Noise

Goal: The student will identify target words in word strings in noise with 90% or greater accuracy.

You will hear some words and some noise. Every time you hear the word _____, raise your hand.

		Dates			
1.	(bag)	tag – wag – rag – *bag* – tag – *bag* – gag – lag nag *bag*			
2.	(fun)	bun – none – sun – run – done – one – *fun* – ton – son – gun			
3.	(mop)	hop – top – *mop* – pop – *mop* – hop – *mop* – top – *mop* – top			
4.	(cat)	rat – bat – at – fat – *cat* – bat – pat – sat – *cat* – rat			
5.	(lip)	sip – rip – dip – *lip* – trip – sip – *lip* – dip – tip – *lip*			
6.	(win)	fin – chin – bin – grin – pin – *win* – sin – tin – grin – bin			
7.	(pit)	sit – it – knit – *pit* – fit – bit – sit – *pit* – it – hit			
8.	(toy)	joy – soy – *toy* – coy – soy – coy – *toy* – joy – coy – *toy*			
9.	(sell)	tell – bell – fell – gel – yell – bell – *sell* – fell – tell – *sell*			
10.	(tack)	jack – sack – *tack* – lack – back – sack – jack – lack – *tack* – pack			
11.	(tick)	lick – pick – wick – kick – *tick* – nick – pick – *tick* – kick – lick			
12.	(saw)	law – jaw – raw – law – claw – jaw – *saw* – thaw – *saw* – law			
13.	(pan)	man – tan – can – fan – tan – *pan* – can – man – ban – fan			
14.	(hole)	roll – dole – toll – *hole* – mole – bowl – roll – coal – pole – *hole*			
15.	(bug)	rug – *bug* – lug – jug – dug – lug – rug – mug – *bug* – hug			
16.	(hum)	yum – bum – some – *hum* – gum – yum – from – bum – *hum* – plum			
17.	(hill)	fill – *hill* – mill – dill – pill – sill – fill – dill – will – *hill*			
18.	(job)	cob – *job* – rob – cob – blob – rob – knob – mob – sob – *job*			
19.	(got)	hot – *got* – pot – rot – *got* – dot – jot – tot – hot – not			
20.	(nap)	lap – tap – zap – *nap* – map – sap – cap – *nap* – zap – tap			
			20	20	20	20
			%	%	%	%

Observations:

Task G: Discrimination of Words in Sentences

Goal: The student will identify target words in sentences in quiet with 90% or greater accuracy.

You will hear a sentence. When you hear the word _____, raise your hand.

			Dates				
1.	(tree)	The boy and girl climbed up the *tree*.					
2.	(bird)	Yesterday, a large *bird* landed in the lake.					
3.	(milk)	His mother left the cookies and *milk* on the table.					
4.	(paper)	The wind was so strong, it blew the *paper* off the porch.					
5.	(pen)	He went to buy new pencils, erasers, and a blue *pen*.					
6.	(leaves)	First they raked, and then they put the *leaves* into a big pile.					
7.	(bread)	The ducks ate the *bread* we threw in the water.					
8.	(door)	The sign said to open the *door* and come in.					
9.	(truck)	The police officer had stopped one *truck* and two cars.					
10.	(dog)	The man walked his *dog* through the park.					
11.	(mouse)	The *mouse* smelled the cheese on the floor.					
12.	(towel)	He dried the dishes with the green *towel*.					
13.	(open)	It was hot, so the teacher had to *open* the window.					
14.	(clock)	Everyone watched the *clock* on New Year's Eve.					
15.	(bush)	The rabbit jumped into the *bush* as we walked by.					
16.	(fin)	The fish had a bright red *fin* and a long tail.					
17.	(neck)	The doctor examined his *neck* for bruises.					
18.	(clap)	The song said to *clap* our hands.					
19.	(knit)	Grandma had enough yarn to *knit* three sweaters.					
20.	(mat)	The children rolled on the *mat* during gym class.					
			20	20	20	20	
			%	%	%	%	

Observations:

Task H: Discrimination of Words in Sentences in Noise

Goal: The student will identify target words in sentences in noise with 90% or greater accuracy.

You will hear a sentence and some noise. When you hear the word _____, raise your hand.

			Dates				
1.	(cat)	The little girl wanted a *cat* for her birthday.					
2.	(hike)	The group went on a *hike* around the lake.					
3.	(mail)	The letter carrier slid the *mail* into the slot in the door.					
4.	(meat)	Dad had to turn the *meat* on the grill.					
5.	(drum)	The band teacher bought a new *drum*.					
6.	(train)	The *train* whistle woke everyone up last night.					
7.	(spoon)	He could not find his *spoon*, so he used a fork instead.					
8.	(chair)	When he stood up, the *chair* tipped over.					
9.	(soap)	The washer had too much *soap* in it.					
10.	(sick)	The family was *sick* for the holidays.					
11.	(school)	After moving, they went to a new *school*.					
12.	(wall)	The ladybug climbed up the kitchen *wall*.					
13.	(book)	The librarian put the *book* back on the shelf.					
14.	(thread)	The sewing machine ran out of *thread*.					
15.	(tigers)	At the zoo, we saw lions, *tigers*, and snakes.					
16.	(swim)	After school was our annual *swim* meet.					
17.	(ghost)	He was dressed as a *ghost* for the play.					
18.	(chips)	They dropped the potato *chips* on the floor.					
19.	(penny)	She found a *penny* underneath the swing.					
20.	(marbles)	The *marbles* were all different sizes and colors.					
			/20	/20	/20	/20	
			%	%	%	%	

Observations:

Task I: Discrimination of Words in Paragraphs

Goal: The student will identify target words in paragraphs in quiet with 90% or greater accuracy.

You will hear a story. Every time you hear the word _____, raise your hand.

	Dates			
1. Juan's Story (leaves) Last fall, my dad and I spent the afternoon raking the *leaves*. We put them into big piles in the middle of our yard. In the evening, I made tunnels in the *leaves* and pretended I was a cave explorer. I had to go inside when it started to rain and the water on the *leaves* got my clothes all wet. When I woke up the next morning, the piles of wet *leaves* didn't seem so fun anymore.				
2. Amy's Story (shoes) I have a special pair of dancing *shoes*. They are pink with ribbons to tie around my ankles. The *shoes* have a hard place where my toes go. My grandma says that's so I can stand on my toes when I dance. She calls them "ballet *shoes*." Everyone in my dance class wears the pink *shoes* too.				
3. Billy's Story (apples) I pass the grocery store every day on the way to school. I like to look at all the *apples* in the window. *Apples* are my favorite food. I like to look at the shiny red *apples*, but I like to eat the sour green ones. I think, someday, I want to grow a tree with lots of *apples*.				
4. Maria's Story (kittens) I think my cat is going to have *kittens*. She eats more food than usual and sleeps all day long. I think that's because making *kittens* makes her tired and hungry. Her stomach looks like it's growing. I think that's where the *kittens* are. I hope the *kittens* come soon.				
5. Jasmine's Story (ice cream) I like chocolate *ice cream*. I like to lick it on a cone two scoops tall. Sometimes, if I don't lick fast enough, the *ice cream* drips on my fingers. Once, I had a cone with chocolate and strawberry *ice cream*. It tasted really good but the *ice cream* fell off the cone into my lap. The next time I got it in a bowl, instead of on a cone.				
	20	20	20	20
	%	%	%	%

Observations:

Task J: Discrimination of Words in Paragraphs in Noise

Goal: The student will identify target words in paragraphs in noise with 90% or greater accuracy.

You will hear a story and some noise. Every time you hear the word _____, raise your hand.

		Dates				
1.	**Adam's Story** (duck) A *duck* lives outside my window. He is black and brown with some green feathers. At school, I saw a picture of a *duck* in the library. Mom says a *duck* usually lives by the water. We live in the city. I think my *duck* is lost.					
2.	**Katie's Story** (raincoat) It's raining outside today. I will have to wear my *raincoat* and hat. My *raincoat* is yellow with black buttons. My sister has a green *raincoat*. When she wears her green *raincoat*, I think she looks like a frog.					
3.	**Amber's Story** (baseball) I like *baseball*. In gym, I get to be the pitcher. I am also pretty good at catching the *baseball* when I play after school. Sometimes I get to watch a *baseball* game on TV. My favorite *baseball* team's colors are black and white.					
4.	**Antoine's Story** (newspaper) I got my first job yesterday. I deliver the Sunday *newspaper*. I get to meet all the neighbors when I give each one a *newspaper*. I also get lots of exercise. I get money for every *newspaper* I deliver. I like to read the headlines of the *newspaper* as I walk from house to house.					
5.	**Jose's Story** (firefighter) When I grow up, I want to be a *firefighter*. My uncle is a *firefighter*. He dresses up in the long yellow coat and drives the fire truck. One time I got to wear his fire hat and pretend to be a *firefighter*. Next time I want to wear the fire boots. I will be a good *firefighter* when I'm older.					
			20	20	20	20
			%	%	%	%

Observations:

References

American Speech-Language-Hearing Association. (2005). (Central) Auditory Processing Disorders. Available at http://asha.org/members/deskref-journals/deskref/default.

Bellis, T.J. (2003). *Assessment and management of central auditory processing disorders in the educational setting (2nd ed.).* Clifton Park, NY: Delmar Learning.

Bradlow, A.R., Kraus, N., & Hayes, E. (2003). Speaking clearly for children with learning disabilities: Sentence perception in noise. *Journal of Speech, Language, and Hearing Research, 46,* 80-97.

Chermak, G.D., Hall, J.W., & Musiek, F.E. (1999). Differential diagnosis and management of central auditory processing disorder and attention deficit hyperactivity disorder. *Journal of the American Academy of Audiology, 10,* 289-303.

Chermak, G.D., & Musiek, F.E. (2002). Auditory training: Principles and approaches for remediating and managing auditory processing disorders. *Seminars in Hearing, 23,* 297-308.

Ferre, J.M. (2004, February). *Definition, diagnosis, and treatment of APD.* Presentation at the Annual Convention of the Illinois Speech-Language-Hearing Association, Arlington Heights, IL.

Gardner, M.F. (1996). *Test of Auditory-Perceptual Skills—Revised. (TAPS-R).* Hydesville, CA: Psychological and Educational Publications, Inc.

Hall, J.W. (2004). *Auditory processing disorders A-12: Management options and approaches* (CD recording). College of Public Health and Health Professions, University of Florida, Gainesville, FL.

Keith, R.W. (1999). *SCAN-C: Test for Auditory Processing Disorders in Children.* San Antonio, TX: Harcourt Assessment, Inc.

RCSLT Clinical Guidelines. Retrieved March 2, 2006, from Royal College of Speech & Language Therapists website: http://www.rcslt.org/resources/clinicalguidelines.

Richard, G.J., & Ferre, J.M. (2006). *Differential screening test for processing.* East Moline, IL: LinguiSystems, Inc.

23-10-9876543

Copyright © 2007 LinguiSystems, Inc.